HORRIBLE SCIENCE

SPECIAL

EXPLOSIVE EXPERIMENTS

NICK ARNOLD

Illustrated by
Tony De Saulles

Hippo

Scholastic Children's Books,
Commonwealth House, 1–19 New Oxford Street,
London WC1A 1NU, UK

A division of Scholastic Ltd
London ~ New York ~ Toronto ~ Sydney ~ Auckland
Mexico City ~ New Delhi ~ Hong Kong

First published in the UK by Scholastic Ltd, 2001

Text copyright © Nick Arnold, 2001
Illustrations copyright © Tony De Saulles, 2001

ISBN 0 439 99927 8

Typeset by Falcon Oast Graphic Art, East Hoathly, Sussex
Printed and bound by Cox & Wyman Ltd, Reading, Berks.

2 4 6 8 10 9 7 5 3

The right of Nick Arnold and Tony De Saulles to be identified as the author and
illustrator of this work respectively has been asserted by them in accordance with
the Copyright, Designs and Patents Act, 1988.

Contents

Nick Arnold has been writing stories and books since he was a youngster, but never dreamt he'd find fame writing about explosive experiments. His research involved testing electric shocks, making his eyeballs wobble and trying to make gold and he enjoyed every minute of it.

When he's not delving into Horrible Science, his hobbies include eating pizza, riding his bike and thinking up corny jokes (though not all at the same time).

Tony De Saulles picked up his crayons when he was still in nappies and has been doodling ever since. He takes Horrible Science very seriously and even agreed to sketch creepy woodlouse experiments. Fortunately, he's not too scared of creepy-crawlies.

When he's not out with his sketchpad, Tony likes to write poetry and play squash, though he hasn't written any poetry about squash yet.

INTRODUCTION

Welcome to *Explosive Experiments*!

This is a book *of* experiments for you to try and also a book *about* experiments and a book about *people* who perform experiments!

And because *Explosive Experiments* is a Horrible Science book you'll be meeting quite a few horrible people, like...

- The man who offered children dog poo to eat.
- The soldier who made his butler dodge bullets.

- The scientist who turned bats into flying fire bombs.

And some *horribly weird* people...

- The scientist who dissolved his own fingertips.
- The engineer who blew up his barbecue.
- The doctor who weighed a tree.

And you'll be finding out about truly *horrible* experiments ... like this one. At Yale University, USA, in 1962 a volunteer was told to give a man in the next room electric shocks. So the volunteer gave the man ever more powerful shocks. Yes, it looked like *torture* and yes, the test seemed to be heading for *murder*!

Now read on...

Deadly Shocks

So what happened next?

Was the man killed by the electric shock? Was the volunteer killed by the scientist?

Well, you'll find out on page 56 – but now it's time to explore the explosive world of experiments. So turn the page – oh, and don't forget your test tubes!

A TESTING TIME

Imagine we're at a science conference. Scientists have come to tell one another about their work, and soon they're happily slurping tea and nattering about science. Then one of the younger scientists comes up with an explosive new idea...

SLUGS ARE SMARTER THAN SPIDERS

But the other scientists disagree...

RUBBISH! DRIVEL! TOSH! BUNKEM!

The argument grows heated and soon a fight breaks out...

STRUGGLE! SQUEEZE! GRAB!

Happily, just in time to avoid bloodshed, a wise and sensible senior scientist makes a sensible and wise suggestion.

STOP!

Yes, experiments can help scientists to check their pet scientific ideas (and avoid scientific punch-ups). A well-planned experiment can show if their cherished ideas are correct or just a load of mouldy old codswallop.

But what exactly is an experiment?

Well, I'm glad you asked me that (as your teacher might say). An experiment is a practical activity designed to test a scientific idea. All experiments have to be carefully watched by scientists who record the results and often repeat tests to check their results.

Experiments are very important for scientists – in the words of US scientist Richard Feynman (1918-1988), who developed a new theory of light...

Think about it ... no matter what your teacher tells you, if it can't be proven by experiment it isn't a proper scientific fact!

9

Explosive expressions

Answer: NO. A hypothesis is the posh word for a scientific idea that hasn't been proven by an experiment.

What's that – you know about experiments already? You've done loads of them in school? OK, so why not check your knowledge with this tricky test?

Strange science quiz

Here are ten experiments (some weren't totally serious). Which *three* are too silly even for the maddest mad scientist (as far as I know).

1) I ran along a pier and leapt into the sea. My work was just a drop in the ocean!

2) We threw cream cakes from a sixth floor window.

3) I zapped electricity through pickle and ate it.

4) I dropped a slice of toast on the floor lots of times.

5) I bungee-jumped in space!

6) We spent ages watching breakfast cereals go soggy.

7) We taught pigeons to tell the difference between the work of different artists.

8) I taught a woodlouse to read.

W IS FOR WOOD

9) We found the chemicals that make dirty, sweaty socks smell cheesy.

10) We got soaked in the rain trying to find out if you stay drier by running or walking to shelter.

Answers:
1 FALSE.
2 TRUE. Students at Rice University, Texas tried this experiment to find the effects of throwing cakes from heights. (It was their idea of a joke.) They found the cake goes *splut!* on the ground and cracks open. Wow, that's really enlightening!
3 TRUE. A group of US engineers at the Digital Equipment Corporation did this. They said the powered-up pickle had a putrid pong – but claimed that it tasted OK. If it had been poisonous they'd have been in a right pickle.
4 TRUE. British scientist Robert Matthews found toast usually falls butter-side down – I hope you're suitably gobsmacked!

5 FALSE. By the way, if you fancy bungee-jumping in space ... you can't. Your body is weightless owing to the effects of orbiting the Earth and you wouldn't actually fall anywhere.

6 TRUE. A team of scientists at Norwich did this in search of what one of them described as "the ultimate breakfast-cereal-eating experience". They ought to try eating cereal on a Monday morning when you're late for school and your dad's in the car revving the engine.

THE ULTIMATE BREAKFAST EXPERIENCE

THE ONE-MINUTE BREAKFAST EXPERIENCE

7 TRUE. Scientists at Keio University, Japan taught pigeons to spot paintings by the artists Picasso and Monet. That's "spot" as in "recognize" not "spot" as in "pesky pigeons plopping on priceless paintings".

8 FALSE.

9 TRUE. A Japanese team did just this! I bet their experiments left them feeling upside-down – geddit? That's right, they had running noses and smelling feet!

10 TRUE. Two American scientists tried this. One walked and the other ran 100 metres. The walking scientist ended up 40 per cent wetter – if there was a competition for silly experiments I'd bet they'd be the "raining" champions.

How it all began

Now at this point you might wonder who invented experiments. Who inspired all these scientists to act strangely? And who's to blame for all those tedious school science experiments? Well, I suppose it all began with an ancient Egyptian king...

Long before anyone had thought of science, people had to try things out by trial and error. You gave something a go – and if it worked it worked and if not, well, it didn't.

The idea of a careful practical test hadn't yet been thought of. But then along came an ancient Egyptian ruler, Pharaoh Psamtiki (663-609 BC). The Pharaoh was curious to learn whether children were born knowing how to talk or whether they needed help. So he ordered two newborn babies to be shut away with no one to talk to. He had set up the world's first experiment. Actually, it was the world's first cruel experiment, but if you were a Pharaoh you could get away with worse deeds than that – in those days life just wasn't fair-oh!

It turned out that the experiment wasn't quite as clever as it appeared. You see, the foolish Pharaoh had forgotten to stop the babies hearing sounds. They heard sheep and started bleating. The woolly-minded King mistook this for talking and thought the babies were chatting in an unknown baby language!

In fact, babies learn to talk by listening to adults and trying to copy them. And so it was that the world's first experiment turned out to be the world's first dud experiment.

It was not to be the last.

For a few hundred years no one tried any experiments and the Pharaoh's fact-finding fix was forgotten. But the idea was so good it was reinvented. In 1269, for example, a French engineer named Pierre de Maricourt (1220-1290) got bored during a war in Italy and did some experiments on magnets. He found that even if you cut a magnet up lots of times it still has two areas where the magnetic force is stronger. We call them the north and south poles – although you probably won't see a polar bear prancing about on a magnet.

(POLAR BEARS ARE ONLY FOUND AT THE NORTH POLE)

Over the next few hundred years records of experiments were as rare as caterpillars who don't like their greens – so let's fast forward to 1583. A teenager named Galileo was sitting in Pisa cathedral, Italy, during an especially boring sermon. Can you imagine the scene? If not, just think of a school science lesson!

A large lantern swung lazily in the breeze and Galileo idly counted its swings. Then, with growing interest, he used his pulse to time the movements and noticed something fascinating. I bet it set his pulse racing! Galileo was a practical lad who enjoyed helping his musician dad tune instruments and as soon as he got home from the cathedral he tried some experiments...

Could you experiment like Galileo?

Here's what Galileo's notebook might have looked like. Could you copy his experiment?

continued →

15

I'll try a little experimento to check this out – I'm sure I'll get into de swing of things!

I took...

A watch with a second hand.

Some Blu-tak, or Plasticine.

46 cm (18 inches) of thread.

What I did...

1 I rolled de ball of Blu-tak 1 cm (0.4 inches) across (just like a ball of my home-made pasta!) and rolled it around one end of de thread to make a pendulum ball.

2 I used more Blu-tak to stick de other end of de thread to de edge of a table.

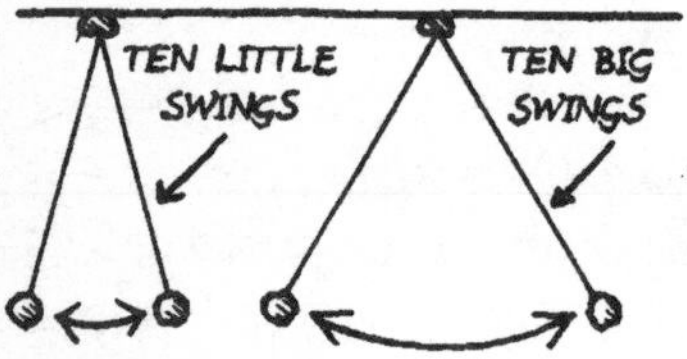

TEN LITTLE SWINGS

TEN BIG SWINGS

3 I swung de pendulum and using my watch timed ten big swings and ten little swings.

Result:

I was eager to know what took longer, de big swings or de little swings. Or maybe they took de same time. I found out that

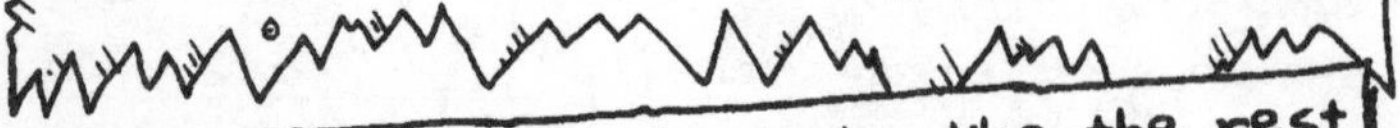

Oops – sorry readers, looks like the rest of the notebook has been lost! If you want to know what happened, you'll have to try the experiment for yourself!

A letter from a famous historian...

Dear Horrible Science,

The so-called notebook of Galileo appears to be a forgery because Plasticine, Blutak and wristwatches hadn't been invented at this time. As I explain in my 596 page biography of Galileo, he used his pulse to time the experiment. Also I should point out

25 PAGES LEFT OUT HERE →

Yours faithfully,
I.B. Vere-Boring

So did *you* discover the result of Galileo's experiment?

Answer:
If the length of the pendulum stays the same every swing will take the same time – no matter how big the swing! This is why if you sit on a swing and swing gently you'll move slowly but when you swing high you'll move faster – try it and you'll see!

LITTLE SWING = SAME TIME AS BIG SWING

Although Galileo had begun the experiment because he was curious about the lantern, he ended up discovering the principle that allows grandfather clocks to keep time.

GRANDFATHER CLOCK KEEPS PERFECT TIME

SWINGING PENDULUM

TICK! TOCK!

THIS GRANDFATHER LOSES TRACK OF TIME

WHAT DAY IS IT?

The experiment finally launched the idea of using experiments to show the laws of science -- a tradition that still inspires scientists today. And all 'cos a youngster got bored – does that mean you'll make a great discovery during a boring science lesson?

Bet you never knew!
People thought you could cook an egg by wrapping it in a scarf and whirling it around your head. This was a daft old story that no one had thought to test. Maybe they reckoned the egg would be cooked by the force of the movement. Although Galileo was a hard-boiled scientist, he actually tried this experiment. Those who believed the story were left with egg on their face when it remained raw.

HERE WE GO...

WHEE!

SHOULD BE COOKED BY NOW...

SPLAT!

Sadly we don't have enough space to tell the story of every boffin who performed an experiment – but there should be a special mention for the scientists who enjoyed showing off their skills in public. Two hundred years ago, going to see an experiment was more popular than going to the cinema (actually that's not so surprising as the cinema hadn't been invented yet).

One place to go was the Royal Institution in London where Michael Faraday (1791-1867) was the big star. Today, Faraday is famous for inventing an early electric motor – but in his day he was famous for his public experiments. In one of them, Faraday stood in a cage with metal-covered bars as 100,000 volts of electricity ran around it. The cage sparked and crackled but the power only ran through the metal and the scientist was safe inside. One spectator, Lady Jane Pollock was electrified with excitement:

> *There was a gleam in his eye that no painter could copy and no poet describe.*

Have you ever seen your science teacher's eyes gleam? (We're not talking about that evil glint that appears just before a science test.)

Now, I bet you're itching to wire up your hamster's cage and throw a few electrical switches, but if you want to act like a real scientist you'll need to experiment properly. So first...

Read these rules
They're so important that we've carved them in stone at great expense to the publishers – and to my toe.

EXPERIMENT RULES

1 Read the experiment instructions before you start.

2. Make sure you've got all the equipment you need.

3. If the experiment is messy always do it outside or on old newspaper.

4. Try to guess the result of the experiment before you start.

5. Don't forget to record your results and try to explain what happened.

6. If the experiment doesn't work try it again There might be a good scientific reason for the failure and you might be the first to discover it!

7. Clean up the mess afterwards or you'll get dirty looks from the rest of the family.

8. Always follow the Safety Code.

ERK!

CRUNCH!

Yes, the *Safety Code*. This is a set of rules so essential that it's become a kind of sacred relic handed down through generations of horrible scientists. Sadly, it's a bit dog-eared now ... but it's still *vital*! So make sure you read this next bit...

~ Ye Olde Safety Code ~

Follow these laws when doing ye experiments and ye shall come to no harm. Break ye laws and ye may suffer death and loss of pocket money.

1 Once ye have mixed ye chemicals or prepared ye experiment always label it so ye family knows what it is. Put it in a safe place out of reach of ye baby brother or sister.

2 When you've finished ye experiment wash ye chemicals down the sink before ye baby brother/sister glugs them down.

3 Always wash ye hands after handling chemicals. Failure to obey this rule may mean ye have to eat ye bar of soap.

4 NEVER NEVER NEVER (ten million more nevers here) use power sockets for ye electricity experiments (including copying Michael Faraday). Ignore this rule and ye may end up like Faraday (that's right – ye will be just as dead as he is).

CONTINUED ▶

5 Get an adult to help with ye cutting, boiling and heating experiments – otherwise ye may end up in hot water.

6 Do not practise ye experiments on brothers, sisters, vicars, parents or family pets without asking them first. (Ye may practise on ye teachers just so long as ye don't inflict too much pain.)

CHEERS!

Look out for the warning signs...

 HORRIBLE FAMILY WARNING!

warns you not to be anti-social.

 HORRIBLE DANGER WARNING!

Tells you what the hazard is and warns you to be ever so C-A-R-E-F-U-L!

 HORRIBLE MESS WARNING!

Warns you of messy experiments.

 HORRIBLE DIFFICULTY WARNING!

tells you when an experiment is getting a bit tricky. You may need to recruit an adult to help with these bits...

Put off yet? Oh well, don't be! Help is on its way...

AN IMPORTANT ANNOUNCEMENT
At vast expense Horrible Science has bribed a team of top scientific experts to show us their laboratory notebooks with experiments you can try yourself! And that's not all – after some friendly persuasion involving large rolls of bank notes they've even agreed to write some experiment quizzes for this book! They'll be popping up later in this book but here's a first chance to meet them:

Dr Grimgrave, the world's most miserable medic.

IS THIS PHOTO REALLY NECESSARY?

HOW MIND-BOGGLINGLY NICE TO MEET YOU!

Professor Funkenstain has spent years on top secret brain experiments.

Dr Will D Beest is an adventurous outdoor face-in-the-dung naturalist.

I'M WILD TO MEET YOU!

HI-YA THERE KIDS!

Miss Esmerelda Perkins is a chemistry teacher and keen experimenter who'll try anything once.

Professor N Large will be enlarging on forces.

GREETINGS!

HELLO EVERYONE!

Wanda Wye is a multi-talented energy and sound expert.

All-round genius Professor Buzzoff is an inventor who studies electricity, magnetism and light, and rumour has it she's an artist.

HELLO — WHAT A WONDERFULLY INTENSE ELECTROMAGNETIC SPECTRUM WE HAVE TODAY!

We'll begin with Dr Grimgrave's medical experiments...
Hey, sssh! Be quiet for a moment – can you hear that noise?

It sounds like blood dripping from the dead bodies in the
next chapter. Yes, it's time to get to drips with grisly, gut-
wrenching human body bits experiments!

MURDEROUS MEDICAL EXPERIMENTS

Guess what? You don't need any complicated equipment for this chapter! You've got everything you need in the shape of one fully functioning, multi-purpose, self-repairing living organism with logic control centre.

IN OTHER WORDS – YOUR BODY!

HUH?

HUH?

HUH?

Doctors, like Dr Grimgrave, know all about how the body works and why it makes revolting noises and smells. But *how* do they know all this? The answer is that all doctors do medical experiments as part of their training and here's some facts about these tests to store in your logic control centre...

Explosive experiments fact file

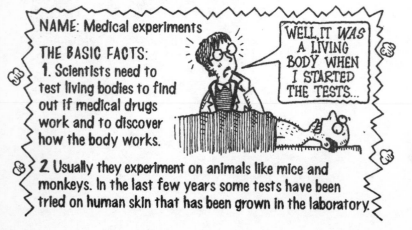

NAME: Medical experiments

THE BASIC FACTS:
1. Scientists need to test living bodies to find out if medical drugs work and to discover how the body works.

WELL, IT *WAS* A LIVING BODY WHEN I STARTED THE TESTS...

2. Usually they experiment on animals like mice and monkeys. In the last few years some tests have been tried on human skin that has been grown in the laboratory.

EXPLOSIVE DETAILS: **1.** Some scientists have performed experiments on their own bodies or on volunteers.

2. But sometimes people were forced to take part in deadly experiments. Read on for the fatal facts...

One of the first scientists to perform medical experiments was a daring doctor who once had to dodge cannon balls. His name was...

Horrible Science Hall of Fame: William Harvey
(1578-1657) Nationality: English

William Harvey was born on April Fool's Day and if that wasn't bad enough he had *six* brothers. Would you want six horrible brothers playing stupid tricks and ruining your birthday?

William studied medicine and as part of his training he went to lectures and watched dead bodies being cut up. This was a popular form of entertainment and people flocked to see the grisly spectacle – oh well, the morgue the merrier.

Eventually William got to be the Royal Doctor to King Charles I of Britain. This was an exciting job because the king was at war with his own parliament and in 1642 William was watching a battle with the king's sons. Cannon balls whizzed uncomfortably close and the doctor and the princes ended up cowering under a muddy hedge.

27

In William's day, doctors believed that blood was made in the liver and ebbed and flowed through the veins like the sea. William was convinced this was a "vein" idea because there was no way the body could make all the blood that passed through the heart in just a few minutes. The blood had to be squirting *around* the body all the time.

Influenced by Galileo (whom he met in Italy), Harvey decided to try some experiments and he worked on them from 1616 to 1628. He cut open living animals but allowed their hearts to carry on beating so he could watch. Sometimes he tied up the blood vessels to watch which way the blood was flowing.

Harvey found that the blood flows out of the heart in blood vessels called arteries and returns in veins, the wider, thin-walled tubes. There's a separate loop that takes the blood from the heart to the lungs and back again before it's pumped around the body. Here's how he might have explained his work...

A bloody science lesson

I squeeze the veins of the arm and blood returns to the heart but it can't move in the other direction. Valves in the veins prevent this.

Ouch — I'm feeling the pinch.

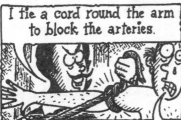

I tie a cord round the arm to block the arteries.

I'm in a tight spot!

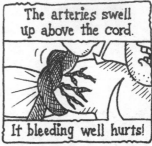

The arteries swell up above the cord.

It bleeding well hurts!

This proves the arteries take blood away from the heart.

I've got a dead arm.

Don't worry — it's an 'armless experiment.

Bet you never knew!

William Harvey's experiments convinced doctors he was right about the blood going round the body. But other scientists had already made the same discovery. Arab doctor Ibn an-Nafus was the first in 1242 (at the time Arab medicine was the best in the world but news of the breakthrough never reached Europe). Later, Italian

Realdo Colombo (1516-1559) and Spanish writer Miguel Servetus (1511-1553) made the same discovery. Servetus fell out with religious leader John Calvin over his religious ideas. Calvin had the scientist arrested, tied to a stake and burnt alive. Let's hope he liked his stake well done.

Scientific villains

Some scientists have performed medical tests on unwilling human victims. During the Second World War German doctors performed revolting and painful experiments on concentration camp prisoners. The victims were told to co-operate or be killed. Experiments included drinking sea water, breathing poison gas and being forced to endure freezing cold.

WANTED FOR MURDER!

Sigmund Rascher

Achievement: Nothing useful to science.

Method: Putting people into chambers in which most of the air was taken out to find out what might happen to a person in a plane at a great height. The victims died after suffering extreme pain.

You might be pleased to learn that, sickened by his evil deeds, Rascher turned against his masters in the ruling Nazi party. He joined an anti-Nazi plot, but in 1944 he was arrested and sent to a concentration camp. No, he wasn't experimented on, but he was executed soon afterwards. Several other scientists involved in the experiments were put to death after Germany lost the war in 1945.

So you'd like to try your hand at a few medical experiments? Well, OK, just so long as you don't use your little brother or sister as a guinea pig.

GUINEA PIG · · · · · · · · · LITTLE BROTHER

Here's a few experiments for you to try from the notebooks of the grumpiest physician ever, Dr Grimgrave. You should know that Dr Grimgrave makes Dr Jekyll and Mr Hyde look like Mr Laurel and Mr Hardy – so no giggles for the rest of this chapter. OK?

MEDICAL EXPERIMENTS
by Dr Grimgrave

· · INTRODUCTION · ·

Disease and death are everyday events for a busy doctor like me. But what bugs me are the idiots who come to see me when they aren't really ill. One day a man said he thought he was invisible – so I told him I couldn't see him today, ha ha. Performing experiments is far more rewarding than dealing with these tiresome time-wasters.

CONTINUED →

CONFUSED TEMPERATURE

What I needed:

● Three bowls: one with hot water from the tap, one with cold water and one with tepid (mixed hot and cold) water. To make it a fair test the bowls must be the same size.

● A watch with a second hand.

⚠ HORRIBLE DANGER WARNING!

HOT WATER FROM THE TAP CAN BE HORRIBLY HOT. THE WATER SHOULD BE COMFORTABLY HOT - NOT SCALDING HOT!

What I did:

1 I dipped one hand in the hot bowl and one hand in the cold bowl for 45 seconds. The cold makes the hand ache a little but cold water never killed anyone. I should know - I start each morning with a bracing cold shower!

2 I placed both hands in the tepid bowl.

Result:

The tepid water felt hot to my cold hand and cold to my hot hand.

HOT! COLD!

Remarks:

Hot and cold feelings are picked up by temperature sensors in the skin. This test proves that the sensors don't always tell you the real temperature. They tell you whether it feels hotter or colder than your skin.

LIAR!

32

ARTIFICIAL SICK

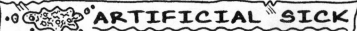

Vomiting is one of the more interesting things my patients do. Artificial sick-making is an instructive scientific activity and it always gives me a good appetite for my supper.

What I needed:

   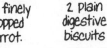

One finely chopped carrot.

2 plain digestive biscuits

100 ml (3.5 fl oz) of water.

50 ml (1.75 fl oz) of vinegar.

50 ml (1.75 fl oz) of milk.

A wooden spoon.

⚠ HORRIBLE DANGER WARNING!

GET AN ADULT TO HELP WITH THE CHOPPING: DR G'S RECIPE SAYS "ONE FINELY CHOPPED CARROT" NOT "ONE FINELY CHOPPED FINGER".

What I did:

1 I poured half the water into the bowl. This represents the saliva (or "spit" as vulgar persons call it) in the mouth.

2 I broke the biscuits into lumps and mixed them with the water. This represents the chewing action of the teeth.

3 Saliva contains a chemical called mucin that makes it stringy. A similar substance is found in milk so I added the milk to the mixture.

4 The acid found in the stomach curdles many foods and gives vomit an interesting appearance. The acid in vinegar has a similar effect so I stirred it in.

33

CONTINUED ➤

5 I added the carrot. Carrots and other tough vegetables can withstand the stomach acid better than softer foods and so carrots are often found in regurgitation. Of course carrots are very healthy - or at least I've never seen a poorly one, ha ha.

VERY FUNNY

I CAN'T EAT THIS, MUM - I'LL BE SICK!

Result:

Some children make fake vomit to get off school. An experienced doctor won't fall for such nonsense and I recommend that children who try this trick should be made to eat their home-made sick. It's for their own good, you know.

BODY HEAT

What I needed:

● Some kitchen foil.
● A large pudding basin.

SHIVER!

● A cool room. (If the room isn't cool the experiment could be performed outside. I keep my consulting room as cold as possible because it saves me money and the patients don't stay so long.)
● A ticking clock or kitchen timer.

What I did:

1 I wrapped the foil (shiny side up) over the inside of the bowl. I took care not to crumple the foil too much (it can be reused - foil costs money you know).

2 I waited until there were no patients

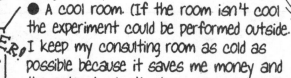

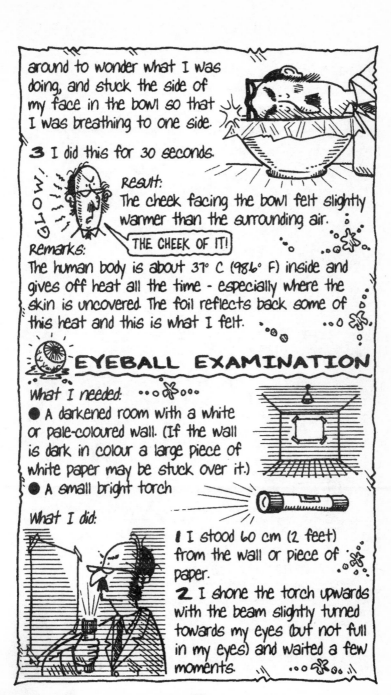

around to wonder what I was doing, and stuck the side of my face in the bowl so that I was breathing to one side.

3 I did this for 30 seconds.

GLOW!

Result:
The cheek facing the bowl felt slightly warmer than the surrounding air.

THE CHEEK OF IT!

Remarks:
The human body is about 37° C (98.6° F) inside and gives off heat all the time - especially where the skin is uncovered. The foil reflects back some of this heat and this is what I felt.

EYEBALL EXAMINATION

What I needed:
● A darkened room with a white or pale-coloured wall. (If the wall is dark in colour a large piece of white paper may be stuck over it.)
● A small bright torch

What I did:

1 I stood 60 cm (2 feet) from the wall or piece of paper.
2 I shone the torch upwards with the beam slightly turned towards my eyes (but not full in my eyes) and waited a few moments.

35

Result:
A fine network of dark channels appeared at the side of my vision.

FASCINATING!

Remarks:
I was looking at the blood vessels inside my own eyeball. They are there all the time of course, but they're made visible by the unusual lighting conditions.
Eyeballs are fascinating bodily structures and I have several in my private medical collection. (I am still looking for a green pair and will swap them for a blue pair.)

TAKING FINGERPRINTS

What I needed:

Some cellophane or see-through plastic.

A magnifying glass.

Some black card.

Some talcum powder.

HORRIBLE MESS WARNING!

This is a messy experiment. Put some newspaper down or you might get fingered with the blame!

RUB!

What I did:
1 I rubbed the underside of one finger over my greasy forehead.

36

2 I pressed the finger on the cellophane.

3 Then I scattered a thin layer of talcum powder over the cellophane and blew it away.

4 Finally, I placed the cellophane over the black card and before studying it further I washed my hands. As a professional medical person I understand the importance of hygiene - I wish I could say the same for some of my smelly patients.

RESULT: My fingerprint showed up clearly and I could study it using the magnifying glass. Here are some features I identified:

ARCH   LOOP   WHORL

REMARKS:
I covered the fingerprint with sticky tape to stop it getting smudged. Last week my favourite fountain pen disappeared and turned up later with its nib broken. I was able to identify the fingerprints on the pen of my colleague, Dr Sneak, who is always losing his cheap nasty biros.

GRRR!

DR SNEAK'S FINGERPRINT

Bet you never knew!
Fingerprints were used to identify people in ancient China but scientists didn't become interested in fingerprints until the 1890s. Then some of the first fingerprint experiments were carried out in Japan. Police forces began to use the new technique and in 1905 they were used in a murder enquiry. Could fingerprints identify the suspects?

The case of the bloody thumbprint
by Chief Inspector Fox ("Fox of the Yard")
London 1905

It was a young boy, William Jones, who made the discovery one rainy March morning. He helped in old Mr Farrow's shop but when the lad arrived for work he found the shop doors were locked. The boy broke in and found the dead bodies of Mr Farrow and his wife: they had been battered to death. Money had been stolen from a cash box and there were two silk masks on the floor.

A little elementary detective work led the police to Alfred Stratton and his brother, two known local villains. Both men were out on the night of the murder, and before the event the younger brother was seen hiding two black masks matching those found at the scene. But this was all the evidence we had linking the brothers to the murders.

I travelled to Tower Bridge police station to interview Alfred. He was a wiry young man, tough-looking and unshaven. I noticed an evil glint in his eyes.

"You won't pin nuffink on me and me bruvver," he declared, folding his arms and gazing defiantly at the green tiled wall. "We ain't done nuffink and I know me rights!"

"You're wrong, Alf," I said. "It's not looking too good for you. You'd best confess and make it easier for yourself."

Alfred spat at me and his face twisted with hatred. "You bobbies is all the same. You make out you're smart but you're a load of 'ot air. Yeah, that's right – you don't know nuffink!"

"You smashed their heads open!" I said, trying to sound tough. But Stratton could see I was bluffing.

"YEAH, RIGHT!" he shouted. "BUT YOU CAN'T PROVE NUFFINK CAN YOU!" And he threw back his head and laughed.

I hurried back to the Scotland Yard with my mind in turmoil. We *had* to find more evidence. Without more proof of their guilt we'd have to release the Strattons and in a city the size of London they could easily disappear for ever.

My superior, Assistant Commissioner Melville Macnaghten, had a visitor with him. Macnaghten was puffing away at his pipe but he motioned me to come in. The visitor was a shabbily dressed fellow with greasy hair, small ears and a huge beard that smelled of sour chemicals. Macnaghten ordered tea from the duty sergeant and whilst it was being prepared he introduced Dr Henry Faulds, a scientist.

"As I was saying," said Faulds self-importantly, "when I was teaching in Japan I saw an ancient pot with the potter's fingerprint preserved in the clay. Well, that's where I got the idea of fingerprinting! I decided to find out whether

fingerprints could be removed. My students helped me and we began by sandpapering the skin off our fingers but the fingerprints grew back. So we tried burning the skin off with acid – again no luck..."

I gazed uneasily at my own fingertips and just then the tea was brought in.

"You mean the prints always grew back?" asked Macnaghten, tugging at the end of his moustache as he always did when something interested him.

"Precisely. So as a final resort we tried dissolving the tips of our fingers using extra-strong acid made from crushed beetles. Again the prints returned."

I imagined crushed beetles floating in my tea. Some of it went the wrong way and I ended up spluttering.

Macnaghten put down his cup with a look of mild distaste and said. "Yes, thank you, Mr Faulds, I think we've heard enough."

But Faulds hadn't finished. "So you see," he continued excitedly, "the technique of fingerprinting was all my doing. Yes, I know others – such as that scientist, Francis Galton – have claimed the credit. But I *suffered* for my experiments! If you could put in a word to your superiors, I am bound to receive my rightful reward..."

"Yes, thank you, Mr Faulds," said Macnaghten firmly. "Now, I'm sure you can see yourself out..."

"But about the reward?" protested Faulds. "I have debts to pay and I'm sure that a few thousand pounds could be found to reward one like myself who..."

"Thank you, Mr Faulds. That will be all."

After Faulds had left, Macnaghten leapt to his feet,

screwed up the notes he had been writing and tossed them into the wastepaper basket. Then he began striding about his office and smacking his palm with his fist.

"This is the third time that Mr Faulds has been in to ask for money!" he remarked. "But I'm sure fingerprints have their uses. A bloody fingerprint was left on the cash box at the murder scene."

My jaw dropped. "I didn't know!" I gasped.

"Phone call from DS Collins, the fingerprint expert at Tower Hill," chuckled Macnaghten, enjoying my surprise. "He rang after you'd left, saying the print matches Alfred Stratton's thumb."

"Well then, sir, we have them!" I exclaimed.

"Not necessarily, Fox. No jury has convicted anyone of murder on the evidence of a fingerprint. They could still walk free and then – who knows? – they might murder some other poor soul."

Macnaghten sat down abruptly, frowning and pressing his knuckles to his lips. And I could see that my boss was still a worried man.

So what happened next?

a) The case was thrown out. The judge said: "I'm not convinced by this newfangled science."

b) The jury found the brothers not guilty. They didn't believe in fingerprints.

c) The Stratton brothers were found guilty and hanged, and the story was front page noose – I mean news.

Answer: c) Henry Faulds told the court that the fingerprint wasn't a perfect match for Alfred Stratton. He was embittered by the refusal of the police to reward his work. But the police experts managed to prove that fingerprints vary according to how hard you press on a surface. The brothers were found guilty and hanged – and all because of an experiment.

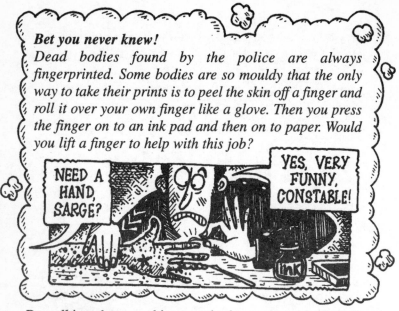

Bet you never knew!
Dead bodies found by the police are always fingerprinted. Some bodies are so mouldy that the only way to take their prints is to peel the skin off a finger and roll it over your own finger like a glove. Then you press the finger on to an ink pad and then on to paper. Would you lift a finger to help with this job?

But talking about working on a body – are you ready to try a few more of Dr Grimgrave's experiments on *your* body? And will you pass Dr G's test?

Dare you discover ... how to test your body?

This is the first in a scintillating series of quizzes written by our experts in which you have to discover the answers by trying the experiments. So why not give them a go? It's what experimenting is all about!

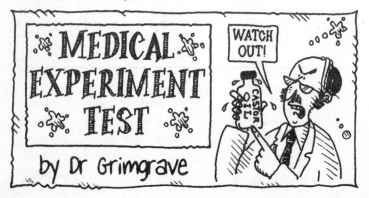

I am setting this test on the assumption that readers will not be allowed to sneak a look at the answers before trying experiments. If I catch anyone cheating I will personally dose them with castor oil - it may taste vile but it's very good for the bowels, you know.

CONFUSING COLOURS

What you need:
Green and red felt tip pens.
Two pieces of white paper.

COLOUR RED

YUMMY NECTAR!

YUMMY INSECT!

COLOUR GREEN

This picture is of an insect-eating plant. (Breeding insect-eating plants was a hobby of mine at one time. They ate the flies - it's a pity they didn't eat my patients too.)

What you do:

1 Place one piece of paper over it and trace the picture.

2 Colour the plant with a red felt-tip pen and the butterfly with a green felt-tip.

CONTINUED →

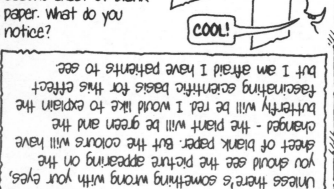

Scientific note

Oh well, I suppose I'd better explain. The retina (the area at the back of your eyeball) has three types of cells – one type sees red, one green and the other blue (all the other colours you see are mixtures of red, green and blue). But if you stare too long at either of these colours the cells switch off and you see the remaining colours instead.

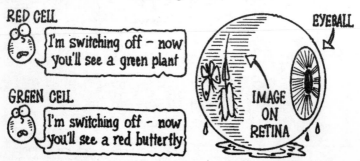

And just in case you're wondering, cells are the microscopic living units that make up your body and all plants and animals. (They're nothing to do with police cells because they're too small to be locked up in.) Now, back to Dr Grimgrave...

HMMMM...

What you need:

A nose and two hands.
(Nose-picking is strictly forbidden during this experiment and at all other times.)

What you do:

1 Hum.

2 Suddenly pinch your nostrils together.
What do you notice?

HMMMM!

HMMMM!

Answer:
The humming stops. Humming involves a rapid wobbling (vibration) is the correct scientific term) of air inside your nose. The air escapes through your nostrils. Pinch your nostrils and you stop this from happening. By humming the right note it's said that you can make your eyeballs wobble slightly (let's hope they don't plop out, ha ha).

WRITE HERE!

What you need:
A fingernail (ideally still attached to a finger).
Your forearm. (The experiment only works if you have pale skin, so if your skin is dark you might need to ask a friend with fair skin.)

What you do:

1 Scratch a word on the underside of your forearm but don't break your skin. In a moment the word appears in the form of white marks.

2 Now rub the skin. What do you notice?

SCRATCH!

RUB!

ANSWER:
The word appears in red! Rubbing the skin scratches away skin cells and makes the skin more see-through. The rubbing also warms blood vessels and causes them to widen. Blood rushes to the area and shows up clearly under the scratched skin. Now, if this experiment makes you a little "funny," I'd advise you to become a comedian and not bother your doctor. Good day to you...

OK, so you've made sick and tested your eyes and tested your skin and tested your nose. But there's one body bit that you haven't got to grips with. Yes, the slippery, bulging mass in the region of the head. No, I don't mean the spot on your brother's forehead – it's the brain I'm talking about.

But is it ready to be *experimented* on?

BAFFLING BRAIN EXPERIMENTS

Perhaps your brain feels like cottage cheese and doesn't know what day it is. Or maybe your mind makes the latest supercomputer look like a brainless stick insect. Either way your brain is your most amazing body bit – and you're about to find out why.

Explosive experiments fact file

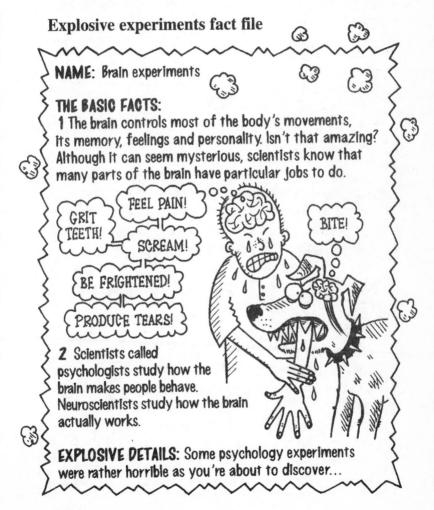

NAME: Brain experiments

THE BASIC FACTS:
1 The brain controls most of the body's movements, its memory, feelings and personality. Isn't that amazing? Although it can seem mysterious, scientists know that many parts of the brain have particular jobs to do.

GRIT TEETH!

FEEL PAIN!

SCREAM!

BE FRIGHTENED!

PRODUCE TEARS!

BITE!

2 Scientists called psychologists study how the brain makes people behave. Neuroscientists study how the brain actually works.

EXPLOSIVE DETAILS: Some psychology experiments were rather horrible as you're about to discover...

Bet you never knew!
In the 1960s scientist Gershon Weltman at the University of California told a group of students they were being lowered 18.3 metres (60 feet) underwater. The students were locked in a sealed chamber called a pressure chamber and given two tasks to work on at the same time. In fact, the chamber didn't go near water. The aim of the experiment was to see how the young people behaved under pressure. (So that's why they called it a "pressure chamber"!) The test showed that people can manage one job when they're worried but only by concentrating so hard that they forget about the second task. Wat-er horrible test!

So is your brain electrified with the thought of experimenting? Here's a never-to-be-repeated peep into the secret notebooks of top brain expert Professor Phoebe Funkenstain. Don't forget to try the experiments yourself and if you want to change your mind, don't worry, the Professor wants to try a few brain transplants – geddit?

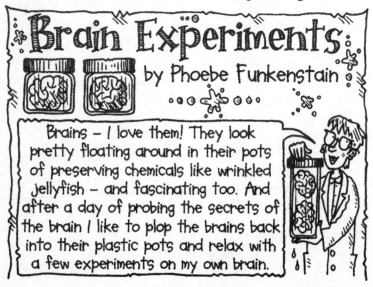

Brain Experiments
by Phoebe Funkenstain

Brains – I love them! They look pretty floating around in their pots of preserving chemicals like wrinkled jellyfish – and fascinating too. And after a day of probing the secrets of the brain I like to plop the brains back into their plastic pots and relax with a few experiments on my own brain.

THE STRANGE CIRCLES MYSTERY

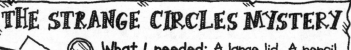

What I needed: A large lid. A pencil. Some coloured paint and brushes. A large sheet of white paper. Some Blu-tak.

⚠ HORRIBLE MESS WARNING!

Messy experiment — put down some newspaper first!

What I did:

1 I drew round the lid with the pencil to make two circles side by side on the paper.

2 I painted one circle a dark colour and the other a light colour. (Purple and a lemony yellow, maybe?)

3 Then I allowed the paint to dry and hung the paper on the wall. I took a few steps back and tried to decide which circle appeared larger.

HMMM!

Result:

Although I knew that both circles were the same size, the lighter circle appeared larger.

Remarks:

For reasons we scientists can't explain, the brain sees light objects as being larger than darker objects. I told my overweight colleague, Dr Bigg, that he would look slimmer in dark colours but did he listen? Dear me – no, he carried on wearing that DREADFUL beige suit!

WHAT'S WRONG WITH BEIGE?

49

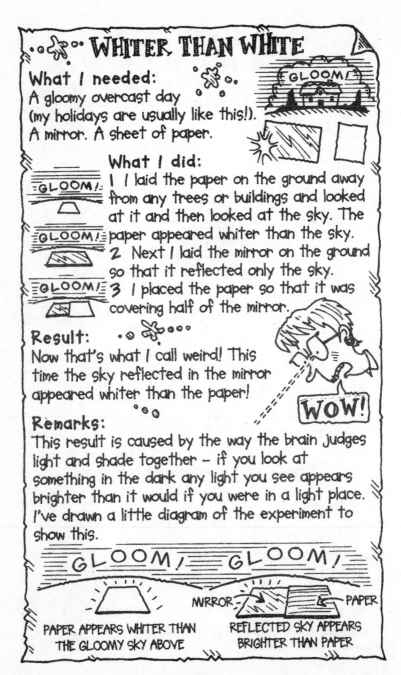

WHITER THAN WHITE

What I needed:
A gloomy overcast day
(my holidays are usually like this!).
A mirror. A sheet of paper.

What I did:
1 I laid the paper on the ground away from any trees or buildings and looked at it and then looked at the sky. The paper appeared whiter than the sky.
2 Next I laid the mirror on the ground so that it reflected only the sky.
3 I placed the paper so that it was covering half of the mirror.

Result:
Now that's what I call weird! This time the sky reflected in the mirror appeared whiter than the paper!

WOW!

Remarks:
This result is caused by the way the brain judges light and shade together – if you look at something in the dark any light you see appears brighter than it would if you were in a light place. I've drawn a little diagram of the experiment to show this.

GLOOM! GLOOM!

MIRROR — PAPER

PAPER APPEARS WHITER THAN THE GLOOMY SKY ABOVE

REFLECTED SKY APPEARS BRIGHTER THAN PAPER

50

SHRINK THE MOON!

What I needed:

A piece of rolled-up paper with a hole 2 cm (0.75 inches) across.
The full moon.

ONE OF THESE

AND ONE OF THESE! →

What I did:

1 I put the roll to one eye and closed the other eye. Then I looked at the moon through the roll.
2 I closed the eye looking through the roll and opened my other eye. Just then the neighbours saw me – lucky they're used to me acting a bit strangely!

Result:

The moon appeared to shrink! I repeated step 2 several times quickly and the moon seemed to grow and shrink.

WEIRD!

Remarks:

Oh dear – yet another brain mystery that we scientists don't understand. One thing we're sure about, though – the moon actually stays the same size! But when the moon is seen next to some closer object it appears bigger than if we see it all by itself.

STRANGE SWINGERS

What I needed:
Some Blu-tak.
42 cm (16.5 inches) of string.
A window.
Some sunglasses.

What I did:
1 I rolled the Blu-tak into a ball 1 cm (0.4 inches) across.
2 I rolled the Blu-tak round one end of the string and used more Blu-tak to hang the string from the top of a window frame inside a room to make a pendulum.
3 Then I set the string swinging and made sure that it was swinging from side to side and not round in a circle.
4 I went to the other side of the room and put on the sunglasses. Next I observed the pendulum, closing first one eye and then the other. Unfortunately I had to stop because the neighbour came round to ask what I was up to the other night.

MIND YOUR OWN BUSINESS

Result:
Seen through my right eye the pendulum appeared to swing around in a circle. Seen through my left eye, the pendulum still swung in a circle – but this time it was moving in the opposite direction! It was enough to make my head spin!

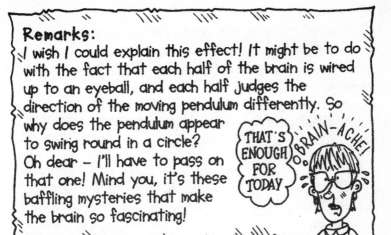

Remarks:
I wish I could explain this effect! It might be to do with the fact that each half of the brain is wired up to an eyeball, and each half judges the direction of the moving pendulum differently. So why does the pendulum appear to swing round in a circle? Oh dear – I'll have to pass on that one! Mind you, it's these baffling mysteries that make the brain so fascinating!

THAT'S ENOUGH FOR TODAY

BRAIN-ACHE!

Mind you, some brain experiments are *more* than fascinating. That's right – they're so horrible they're *horribly* fascinating!

Could you be a psychologist?

US scientist Paul Rozin wants to know how the brain reacts to disgusting things. His experiments include asking little children to eat a plate of dog poo and drink a glass of apple juice with a dead cockroach floating in it.

How do the children react?

a) One little girl threw up over the scientist.

SPEW!

FASCINATING!

b) The children wouldn't touch the meal but a baby happily ate the dog poo.

CHOMP!

CHOKE!

c) One little boy actually drank the apple juice and swallowed the cockroach by mistake.

Answer: b) Don't be shocked – the "dog poo" turned out to be a lump of chocolate fudge cake shaped like dog poo, so no wonder the baby scoffed it! The experiments seem to show that children don't understand about disgusting things until they're about four. Award yourself half a point for c) because a seven-year-old boy did drink the apple juice but only after the cockroach had been fished out.

Would you do this?

But that experiment wasn't as cruel as one by US psychologist Philip Zimbardo. In 1971, Zimbardo turned part of the University of California into a prison. (What d'ya mean he could have used your school?) The scientist wanted to see how people would react to the experience of being prisoners or guards. Here's how two of the volunteers might have told their stories.

Banged up!

The experiment ended when the scientist's girlfriend visited the prison and burst into tears at the suffering of the prisoners. For example, they were only allowed to use the toilet when blindfolded – which must have been messy. I hope your prison – er, place of education – isn't this bad!

Some scientists said the experiment wasn't useful because the university wasn't a real prison and everyone was acting a part. But others suggested that the test showed that given the chance ordinary people can be cruel to one another. But one experiment in cruelty had already gone further ... much, *much* further. Remember the story at the beginning of this book about the electric shocks? Still wanna know what happened next?

OK, let's begin at the beginning...

Deadly Shocks

Yale University, USA 1962

The three men sat on comfy chairs. The volunteer, Joseph Hanna, was a smartly dressed businessman and he had just shaken hands with a second man who had introduced himself as an accountant.

"Hey – I'm a volunteer too," smiled the stranger, a plump man in his forties.

And now they were listening to the third man, a stern-faced scientist with hair the colour of iron. "The experiment measures the effects of punishment on learning, and I expect you to obey my orders at all times.

DO YOU UNDERSTAND?

The volunteers nodded and agreed to pick cards to decide who was to help the scientist and who would be the learner.

The accountant chose a two of spades. "Just my luck!" he shrugged.

Hanna picked out a king of hearts.

The scientist led the accountant to a small booth. He strapped the man to a chair and wired his arm to an electrode. Then he showed Hanna into an adjoining room with a switchboard. Each switch was labelled and Hanna read the labels with growing unease.

The scientist ordered Hanna, to sit at the control desk.

"Your job," he told Hanna "is to administer shocks. Each time the learner gets a question wrong you must increase the voltage."

Hanna blinked rapidly. "But don't the shocks hurt?" he enquired.

"They're meant to hurt," said the scientist, "but there won't be any scarring. Now give yourself a small shock to test the system. You must place that electrode on your arm."

Hesitantly Hanna did as he was told and the scientist pressed down the "slight shock" switch. There was a click and a loud buzz like an angry wasp. A jolt of pain ran up Hanna's arm.

"Ouch!" he cried. The experiment had begun.

The accountant proved a poor learner. He often gave wrong answers and, each time he did, the scientist ordered an increasingly alarmed Hanna to inflict a more powerful shock. Hanna felt he was in a dream. *In a moment*, he thought, *I'll wake up.*

The accountant was brave: he stayed silent except for the odd grunt. Then suddenly he yelled:

STOP! I CAN'T STAND THE PAIN! I REFUSE TO GO ON!

"You *must* answer my questions!" said the scientist, and the lines around his mouth deepened. Hanna gave him a worried look; his heart was pounding and his mouth was dry.

"And as for you, Mr Hanna," said the scientist coldly. "You are also expected to complete the experiment. You cannot stop now."

Hanna pulled at his earlobe and fiddled with his tie and clasped his sweaty hands to stop them shaking. But the scientist was standing at his shoulder, urging him to hurry up and flick the switch. They heard the accountant scream with pain and kick the booth. He begged to be let out but he answered the scientist's questions. He was still co-operating.

Hanna's mind filled with objections but he dared not speak. Then suddenly there was silence, the scientist's questions met with no reply.

They had reached the final switch.

"The learner is refusing to answer. He must be punished," said the scientist.

Hanna tried to argue, but the scientist yelled at him.

And so Hanna moved to press the switch.

Suddenly he froze. "I can't do it," he said in stricken tones.

"You *must* do it!" growled the scientist.

"I'm sorry, I'm sorry!" said Hanna quietly and he buried his face in his hands. He had never felt so bad. Tears trickled through his fingers and his breath came in little gasps.

"I am going to leave the room," said the scientist. "And when I return I expect you to have flicked that switch."

Hanna blew his nose, clumsily wiping sweat and tears from his pale face. Suddenly he had an idea. He reached out and quickly flicked the "slight shock" switch. The machine clicked and buzzed but there was no response from the victim.

"OK, hey – come back – I've done it!" Hanna called weakly.

"Very well," said the scientist, returning. His voice sounded calmer now, more gentle. He took the weak-kneed Hanna by the arm and steered him into the next room.

"I thought you might like to see the learner," he said.

Hanna imagined the crumpled body. He didn't want to look and he scarcely dared breathe. But the accountant was lounging in his booth with his feet up on the shelf in front of his chair.

"Hi there," he called, his mouth full of doughnut. "Great experiment. Hey, pal, you look awful. Have some coffee!"

The scientist's cheek twitched, it was obvious that he was quietly amused.

"He, he's alive!" stammered Hanna in disbelief.

"Yes," agreed the scientist with a bleak smile, "he's an actor. The whole thing was a set-up."

The experiment had been designed by scientist Stanley Milgram to show how far people were prepared to obey orders. Other scientists complained about the cruelty of the tests but they were stunned to learn that over 60 per cent of the volunteers had agreed to inflict pain on another person.

Dare you discover ... how your brain works?

So you wouldn't mind testing your own brain (just so long as there are no electric shocks involved)? Well, that's great because Professor Funkenstain has written a quiz just for you!

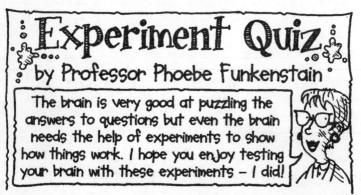

Experiment Quiz

by Professor Phoebe Funkenstain

The brain is very good at puzzling the answers to questions but even the brain needs the help of experiments to show how things work. I hope you enjoy testing your brain with these experiments – I did!

A TUBE WITH A VIEW

What you need:
A dim but not dark room (draw the curtains if it's daytime).
A long narrow cardboard tube – 30 cm (12 inches) long and 2 cm (0.8 inches) wide is ideal.

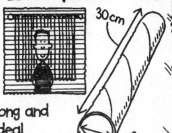

30 cm

2 cm

FREAKY!

What you do:
Put the tube to one eye but keep both eyes open. What do you notice?

Answer:
A light circle appears before your eyes – it's actually the view through the tube. Confused? Well, it's all to do with that fact on page 50 – the darker the surroundings, the brighter a light area will appear to your brain. So by looking down the dark tube you make the view at the end of the tube appear brighter. Oh well, it's nice to look on the bright side of life!

FINGER WAGGLE

What you need:
A finger. (It's best to use your own although I did use one that had been removed from a dead body once.) Your eyes and brain would be useful too.

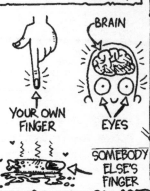

YOUR OWN FINGER

BRAIN

EYES

SOMEBODY ELSE'S FINGER

What you do:
1 Hold your index finger loosely upside-down up to the light.
2 Waggle the finger as quickly as possible from side to side.

What do you notice?

WAGGLE!

Answer:
A second finger appears! It's caused by the delay between your eyeball seeing the finger and your brain picking up the image. The delay is only half a second but it means that your finger is moving too fast for your brain to follow it and so you see two images of your finger. Did you have to think twice about this experiment?

AN A-DOOR-ABLE EXPERIMENT

What you need:
A doorway.
Two arms.
A ticking clock or kitchen timer.

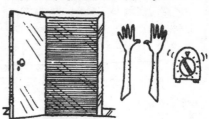

Me

What you do:
1 Stand in the doorway with your arms outstretched and pointing downwards and with your hands pressing upwards and outwards against the doorframe.

62

2 If the doorway is too wide ask an adult to hold the door open with their foot at a suitable distance. Then place yourself between the door and one side of the frame.

3 Push your hands upwards as hard as you can for 20–30 seconds.

PRESS!

RELAX! RELAX!

4 Relax your arms and let them hang loosely by your sides.

What do you notice?

THANKS DAD!

Answer: Your arms rise up on their own! This is because your brain is still sending nerve signals telling your arms to rise up. Now isn't that strange?

So your arms are aching? You think that experiment was a bit hard on you? Oh well, cheer up – you can relax in the next chapter because it's full of cute fluffy little animals!

GROWL!

Er, maybe not...

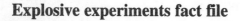

NIGHTMARE NATURE EXPERIMENTS

In the interests of science, some people endure hours of discomfort and boredom followed by extreme terror as they're savaged by a cruel, bloodthirsty creature. Yes, biology lessons can be a little bit tough: but then so are biologists. Anyway, here's the essential info on their experiments...

Explosive experiments fact file

NAME: Biology experiments

THE BASIC FACTS: Biology is the science of living things. Biology experiments can solve particular problems like testing animal senses, or studying how plants grow under coloured light.

DER!

ANIMAL WITH VERY LITTLE SENSE

EXPLOSIVE DETAILS: One early plant experiment was by Flemish doctor Jan van Helmont (1579–1644). Jan wanted to know how plants grew, so he grew a willow tree and weighed it at regular intervals. He thought that watering made the tree heavier.

"WATER" BRILLIANT DISCOVERY!

WRONG! - Actually the weight gain was due to the chemical, carbon. The carbon came from carbon dioxide drawn in through the leaves. If Jan had known he'd have felt like a weeping willow.

Dare you discover ... getting to grips with plants?
So you wouldn't make such a basic mistake? OK, well our nature expert Will D Beest has set you two easy plant experiments to try. And you'll have to try them to come up with the answers!

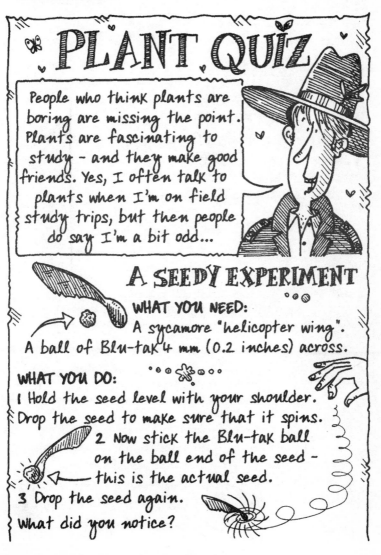

PLANT QUIZ

People who think plants are boring are missing the point. Plants are fascinating to study – and they make good friends. Yes, I often talk to plants when I'm on field study trips, but then people do say I'm a bit odd...

A SEEDY EXPERIMENT

WHAT YOU NEED:
A sycamore "helicopter wing".
A ball of Blu-tak 4 mm (0.2 inches) across.

WHAT YOU DO:
1 Hold the seed level with your shoulder. Drop the seed to make sure that it spins.
2 Now stick the Blu-tak ball on the ball end of the seed – this is the actual seed.
3 Drop the seed again.
What did you notice?

65

Answer:
This time the seed falls to the ground without spinning. The weight of the wing and the seed have to balance for it to spin. When the sycamore seed forms on the tree it's green and full of moisture but the sensible sycamore doesn't let it go until it's dry and lighter and ready to spin through the air. Try to see it from the tree's point of view: it wants its seeds to fly a good distance away where there might be more water and light. Isn't that thoughtful!

MIX 'N' MATCH

WHAT YOU NEED:
A spent match.
Your hand, complete with fingers.

⚠️ HORRIBLE DANGER WARNING!

Don't even think of striking the match yourself. Get an adult to do it — that way they can risk burning holes in their underwear!

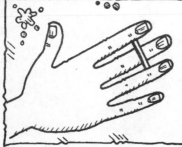

WHAT YOU DO:
1 Place the match over your middle finger and under your second and fourth fingers as shown.

2 Try to break the match. What did you notice?

Answer: It's hard to do – you may find that you can't do it! You see, matches are made from wood (please don't faint in surprise) and wood is very strong. Wood is made of strong bendy fibres of a substance called lignin – and guess what? As I write this my bum is resting on some lignin!

LIGNIN CHAIR
ME
A FRIEND

Could you be a botanist? (That's a plant scientist, by the way.)

In 1969, scientist Dorothy Retallack tested whether music affects how a plant grows. She grew corn, squash (that's a type of vegetable, not the fruit drink) and marigolds.

What did she find?

a) Plants are cool and funky and enjoy the latest chart hits.

b) Plants are seriously old-fashioned – they like boring old fuddy-duddy classical music. Rock music kills them off!

c) Plants are unaffected by music. (Maybe that's because they're deaf – all except for "ears" of corn, ha ha.)

Answer: b) When plants were exposed to rock music their leaves and roots were shorter, and the weedy little marigolds actually died.

Bet you never knew!
In Yorkshire, England, there's a special research centre where scientists test ... grass. It's true – every day you can see dedicated boffins kicking balls around to test the suitability of various types of grass for football pitches. Rumours that the scientists are having fun kickabouts are entirely unfounded.

MAN ON!

ON ME 'ED, SON!

OFF-SIDE!

NOTE FROM AUTHOR – *I THINK THIS MUST BE SCIENTIFIC LANGUAGE DESCRIBING THE CONDITION OF THE GRASS

You might like to try these kinds of experiment for yourself – but now for some nature experiments you definitely *shouldn't* try...

Two very nasty nature experiments

1 Blind bats

In the 1700s no one knew how bats could fly in the dark without bumping into things. So Italian scientist Lazaro Spallanzani (1729-1799) caught some bats in the tower of Pavia Cathedral and blinded them. Some of the unlucky bats had plugs stuffed in their ear holes as well. The batty boffin found that the bats could fly without seeing but with their ears blocked up they kept bumping into things. This proved that sound helps bats find their way even when the bats are as blind as ... er ... bats. Scientists now know that bats can judge the echoes from their calls to avoid bashing a-bat in the dark.

2 Exploding bats

Sorry, bat lovers, but during the Second World War US scientist Dr Louis Feisner planned to strap fire bombs to thousands of bats and drop them on Japanese cities. Of course this was an un-squeakable idea. Here's what happened next...

Mad as a bat

The bats will crawl under overhanging roofs and set them on fire.

BUT THE EXPERIMENTS DIDN'T GO ACCORDING TO PLAN...

Where have all the bats gone?

They've flown back to the aircraft hanger, Dr F!

What about the bombs?

The bombs were on the bats.

BOOM!

Oh no, here comes the General!

How's it going, Feisner?

Well, the bombs work fine...

Please, sir!

Don't interrupt me...

A testing question

Our two examples just happen to have been about bats. But in fact scientists have performed thousands of experiments on animals – mostly mice and rats but also cats and dogs and monkeys and just about any other creature you can think of. Some experiments are to do with how animal bodies work, others are tests of drugs or foods to find out if they're safe for humans.

Most countries have strict rules controlling animal experiments. The rules aim to stop the animals from suffering unnecessary distress, but animal lovers say that any test on an animal is cruel. The scientists reply that they have to perform animal experiments because there's no other choice and some tests could save human lives.

So what do you think about animal testing?

Well, while you're deciding, let's get on with the story of nature experiments. In the 1880s scientists became interested in animal intelligence. This new branch of science was pioneered by a scientist who had some rather wild ideas...

Horrible Science Hall of Fame: George Romanes
(1848-1893) Nationality: British

George was a rich, rather spoilt kid who enjoyed a wild life with wildlife, just so long as this involved blasting birds with a gun. But at university he became interested in science and jellyfish nerves and spent ages cutting up jellyfish to find out how they move. (He thought that jellyfish don't have nerves – they do, but George didn't spot them. Maybe his nerve failed, ha ha.) He became fascinated by animal brains and attempted some wacky experiments. He described these in a book and this might just be an extract...

Animal Intelligence
by George Romanes

Chapter 1 ~ *MINDLESS MOGGIES*

Cats are dim! I've proved this by an experiment: I borrowed some cats from their owners and let them loose on Wimbledon Common, London. The cats ran off in all directions. If the fur-brained felines had any intelligence they'd have found their way home – but so far none have. Then the

owners wanted to know where their pets had got to — so I had to do a disappearing act myself.

SCIENTIFIC NOTE

The cats were confused at being in a strange place. This experiment proved nothing.

Chapter 2 – *MONKEY BUSINESS*

I was keen to study how monkeys behave, so I arranged for my sister to look after one in her own home.

"I'll pay for any damage," I promised.

Well, I didn't know the monkey would trash the place, did I? We found that the monkey got jealous when my sister pretended to feed a toy monkey and it thought its reflection in a mirror was another monkey. This proves that monkeys get jealous and they aren't too clever (unlike an

all-round genius like me). Then my sister started talking about the bill and I went off on a long field trip to a remote part of the country.

SCIENTIFIC NOTE

Nowadays scientists aren't so interested in how intelligent animals are. They're more concerned with how animals live in the wild and how the animals' brains help them to do this.

Meanwhile, scientists were also experimenting with plants and one Austrian scientist had achieved a breakthrough that changed the entire world. The trouble is that no one noticed! But we are very proud to present the very amazing and very dead Gregor Mendel who has been dug up for an exclusive interview.

Dead brainy: Gregor Mendel (1822-1884)

How does it feel to be dead? I could do with a stiff drink.

And what would you be doing if you were alive today?

Trying to get out of my coffin.

You're famous for discovering what we now call genes. How did you make this discovery.

I was a monk and worked in the monastery garden. I decided to explain why some plants produced wrinkled peas and some had smooth peas. So I planted thousands of pea plants...

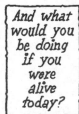

Was it tiring?

Sometimes I was dead on my feet. In fact, I still am...

I realized that every pea plant carried two sets of instructions which could be one of these...

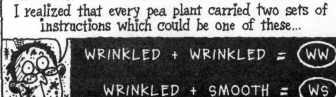

WRINKLED + WRINKLED = (WW)

WRINKLED + SMOOTH = (WS)

SMOOTH + SMOOTH = (SS)

73

If the "smooth" instructions were there at all, the peas were smooth. When the peas were wrinkled this meant the plant had two sets of "wrinkled" instructions. This happened in one in four plants.

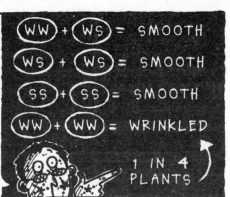

WW + WS = SMOOTH
WS + WS = SMOOTH
SS + SS = SMOOTH
WW + WW = WRINKLED

1 IN 4 PLANTS

How on earth did you prove that?

I counted up thousands of peas.

What do you say to modern scientists who claim that you fiddled your figures to get that one in four result.

Grr — they should mind their "peas and q's"!

What do you say to claims that you started calling the pea plants your "children" and went crazy?

But the plants started calling me "Dad". Yibble, yibble...

Sadly when Gregor announced his dramatic result, the fruit – or should I say the vegetable – of years of painful labour, he was ignored by pea-brained scientists. So he gave up experiments. Forty years later scientists realized that Gregor's pea instructions were what we called genes and in 1953 scientists worked out how genes are stored in the chemical DNA found inside cells.

In 2000, scientists announced that they had worked out the entire series of genes for a human being, a discovery that opened the door for more work on diseases caused by faulty genes. Clearly poor old Gregor was a gene-uine gene-ius. Are you one too? Here's your chance to prove that you're a *natural* scientist...

Could you be a naturalist?

1 In 1748, French scientist Jean-Antoine Nollet (1700-1770) was studying cells (remember that word from page 45?). He filled a pig's bladder with alcohol and placed it in some water. What happened next?

a) The bladder exploded (no doubt splattering the scientist with unmentionable substances).

b) The bladder shrank.

c) The bladder turned itself inside-out.

> **Answer: a)** Like all cells the cells in the bladder had walls with tiny holes that let in water but not alcohol. So no alcohol escaped from the bladder, but it sucked in water until it went *pop!*

75

2 In 1994, a man in Arizona tested whether he could cure a rattlesnake bite with electric shocks. What did he do?
a) He let the snake bite a rat, then gave the rat a shock.
b) He let the snake bite his arm and gave himself a shock.
c) He let the snake bite his son's teacher and gave the teacher an electric shock.

Answer: b) The treatment was as useless as it was painful, and the man needed emergency treatment for the bite.

3 In 1994, US scientist Robert Lope experimented to see whether cat ear mites can live in the ears of humans. He placed some mites in his own ears. What happened?
a) He developed a curious craving for cat food.
b) He went deaf for a while.
c) The mites got stuck in his ear wax and died.

Answer: b) The scientist heard the tiny bugs scratching about in his ear and experienced itching and pain and deafness for a while. To check his results the scientist bravely repeated the test – *twice!*

4 American scientist R L Solomon wanted to see if puppies had a conscience. He put them in a room with a plate of their favourite snack (boiled horsemeat) and some cheapo doggie food. The puppies made for the horsemeat but a grumpy scientist whacked them away with a rolled-up newspaper and the poor puppies had to make do with nasty dog food. Solomon repeated the test every day for a week. The next morning the puppies were left alone with the two bowls of food – what did they do?

a) They gobbled the horsemeat.

b) They ate the doggie food because they knew that's what the scientist wanted them to do.

c) They chewed the scientist's newspaper and peed in his slippers.

*NEXT TIME WE'LL POOP IN YOUR POCKETS!

Answer: b) Most of the puppies ate the doggie food – but some naughty puppies guzzled the horsemeat. The scientist claimed that most puppies have a conscience. Can you imagine a similar experiment that gave a group of children the choice between eating a school dinner and scoffing a big bag of choccies?

And if that encourages you to try some more nature experiments, here's your chance. Yes, it's time to inspect Dr Will D Beest's notebooks.

I wonder what we'll find inside?

A WALK ON THE WILD SIDE
by Will D Beest

I've been studying wild rabbits on a remote island in the South Atlantic. Oh well, it gave me something to rabbit about to my fellow scientists. Anyway, when I got back I had to look after my horrible little nephew, Wayne. Wayne and I tried these experiments, but after a week of Wayne I was wishing I was back on that island!

HOW I MADE FRIENDS WITH A WOODLOUSE (BUT NOT MY NEPHEW)

WHAT I NEEDED:

LITTLE PAL

LITTLE PEST

TEE HEE!

A WOODLOUSE

WAYNE

BLACK INSULATING TAPE

A JAM JAR, WITH TAPE ROUND THE UPPER HALF

WHAT I DID:

1 Wayne caught a woodlouse. (The best place to look is under rotting wood or stones in a damp corner of the garden. Wayne caught six more and I later found them in my bed.) I put the woodlouse in the bottom of the jar. Luckily I'm not scared of ugly little creatures (just certain little kids). Then I replaced the lid.

UNDER HERE

2 I placed the jar at a slight angle. (I made sure the slope was gentle enough to allow the little beastie to struggle up the glass.)
3 Then Wayne and I watched what the woodlouse did next...

LITTLE BEASTIE

BLOB OF BLU-TAK

RESULT:

The woodlouse struggled up the slope into the dark area. I repeated the experiment a few times and then asked Wayne to put my new friend back where he found him. Yes, woodlice have feelings too you know. Unlike my nephew... Hey, Wayne, not down my neck!

REMARKS:

It would have been easy for the woodlouse to stay at the bottom of the jar but woodlice always head for dark places. They want to hide from larger creatures and from the sun which can dry their little bodies out. I suppose they're shady characters, ha ha.

VERY PUNNY

SNAIL SHELL STRENGTH TEST

HORRIBLE MESS WARNING!

This experiment can be messy — it's best done outside.

WHAT I NEEDED:
AN EMPTY SNAIL SHELL. (THE SHELL MUST BE EMPTY BECAUSE IT'S GOING TO BE CRUSHED AND CRUSHED SNAILS ARE MESSY.)

EMPTY   NOT EMPTY

A SET
OF
SCALES

A LARGE
PUDDING
BOWL

A
GLASS

SOME
FINE
SAND OR
SUGAR

A CALCULATOR
(FOR PEOPLE
LIKE ME WHO
HATE SUMS).

WHAT I DID:

1 I weighed the bowl and then the glass. I noted down these figures before I forgot them!

2 Then I filled the glass with sand and weighed it again, once more noting the weight.

Hmm – I had to take away the weight of the empty glass from the weight of the full glass to work out the weight of the sand in the glass.

3 I put the snail shell on the ground and placed the bowl on top of it. I needed a few bricks on either side to hold the bowl in position (but not to support it).

4 Then a glassful at a time I began to add sand to the bowl. I tried to pour it slowly and Wayne counted how many glassfuls I poured into the bowl. Hey, Wayne, have you put sand in my tea?

RESULT:
After several glassfuls the shell suddenly shattered into bits. Then I did this sum...

| NUMBER OF GLASSFULS (INCLUDING THE ONE I WAS JUST POURING) | × | WEIGHT OF SAND IN ONE GLASSFUL | − | THE AMOUNT OF SAND LEFT IN THE GLASSFUL I WAS JUST POURING | + | THE WEIGHT OF THE BOWL | = | **ERK!** THE WEIGHT NEEDED TO BREAK A SNAIL SHELL |

REMARKS:

Snail shells might be thin but they're certainly not weak. My shell took 1.83 kg (4 lbs) before it smashed – that's over 60 THOUSAND times the shell's weight. It's like plonking 4,500 tonnes on top of Wayne and not squashing him. (Now there's a nice thought!)

WAYNE

SNAIL SHELL FIZZ

I had a few messy bits of snail shell left over from the last experiment. But I knew a way to get rid of them!

WHAT I NEEDED:

A ROLLING PIN

SOME BITS OF SNAIL SHELL

A MEASURING JUG CONTAINING 50 ML (1.7 FL OZ) OF VINEGAR.

A BOWL

WHAT I DID:

1 I put the snail shell bits into the bowl and Wayne kindly crushed them into the smallest, tiniest pieces he could with the end of the rolling pin. OK, Wayne, that's enough crushing!

2 I poured the vinegar over the snail shell bits and left them for 30 minutes.

RESULT:
X-RAY VIEW OF BOWL ➔

The liquid was full of tiny bubbles.

REMARKS:

These bubbles are carbon dioxide gas made by a chemical reaction between a chemical called calcium carbonate in the shell and the vinegar. Or to put it more simply – the vinegar is dissolving the shell.

SCIENTIFIC NOTE

Teachers use calcium carbonate to write on blackboards. And yes, you're right – the experiment proves that snails have chalky shells.

EYES AT THE SIDES OF YOUR HEAD

HORRIBLE DANGER WARNING!

This experiment involves cutting – get an adult to help! No, I don't care if they're busy watching telly!

WHAT I NEEDED:
A PIECE OF METALLIC SHINY CARD FROM AN ART SHOP. (IF I HADN'T FOUND THE SHINY CARD, I WOULD HAVE CUT ORDINARY CARD TO SIZE AND USED STICKY TAPE TO STICK KITCHEN FOIL OVER IT.)

SOME SCISSORS

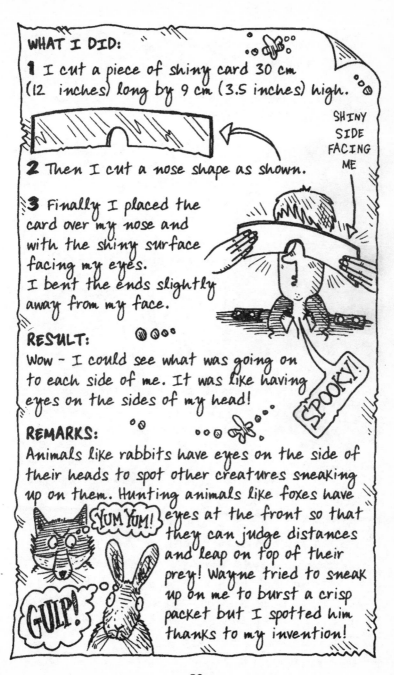

WHAT I DID:

1 I cut a piece of shiny card 30 cm (12 inches) long by 9 cm (3.5 inches) high.

SHINY SIDE FACING ME

2 Then I cut a nose shape as shown.

3 Finally I placed the card over my nose and with the shiny surface facing my eyes. I bent the ends slightly away from my face.

RESULT:

Wow — I could see what was going on to each side of me. It was like having eyes on the sides of my head!

SPOOKY!

REMARKS:

Animals like rabbits have eyes on the side of their heads to spot other creatures sneaking up on them. Hunting animals like foxes have eyes at the front so that they can judge distances and leap on top of their prey! Wayne tried to sneak up on me to burst a crisp packet but I spotted him thanks to my invention!

YUM YUM!

GULP!

THE SHIVERING BANANAS EXPERIMENT

(Actually, bananas don't shiver but you'll see the reason for this title in a moment.)

WHAT I NEEDED:
Three yellow bananas from the same bunch.

WHAT I DID:

1 One banana was put in the freezer. One went into the fridge. One was left out in the kitchen.

2 I left the experiment for a week. I had to put warning signs on my bananas after the dreaded Wayne scoffed the first lot! (One day I'll take him on a one-way trip to study the feeding habits of man-eating crocodiles.)

3 Then I compared the bananas.

RESULT:

1 Within one hour the banana in the freezer was deep yellow and rock hard. It didn't change in a week. I removed the frozen banana from the freezer and within an hour it had turned black and was oozing brown juice – yuck! Inside, the banana was mushy but not smelly.

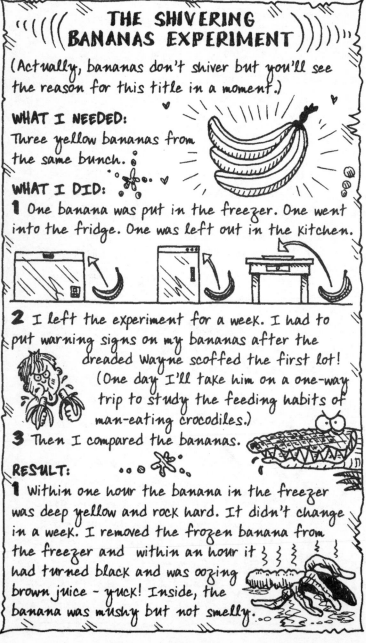

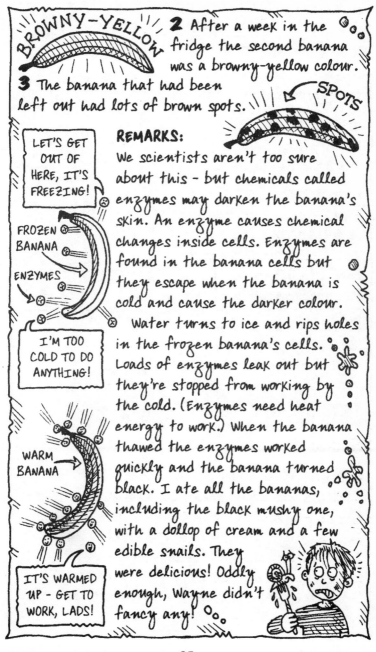

BROWNY-YELLOW

2 After a week in the fridge the second banana was a browny-yellow colour.

3 The banana that had been left out had lots of brown spots.

SPOTS

REMARKS:

We scientists aren't too sure about this – but chemicals called enzymes may darken the banana's skin. An enzyme causes chemical changes inside cells. Enzymes are found in the banana cells but they escape when the banana is cold and cause the darker colour.

Water turns to ice and rips holes in the frozen banana's cells. Loads of enzymes leak out but they're stopped from working by the cold. (Enzymes need heat energy to work.) When the banana thawed the enzymes worked quickly and the banana turned black. I ate all the bananas, including the black mushy one, with a dollop of cream and a few edible snails. They were delicious! Oddly enough, Wayne didn't fancy any!

LET'S GET OUT OF HERE, IT'S FREEZING!

FROZEN BANANA

ENZYMES

I'M TOO COLD TO DO ANYTHING!

WARM BANANA

IT'S WARMED UP – GET TO WORK, LADS!

BUBBLING IVY

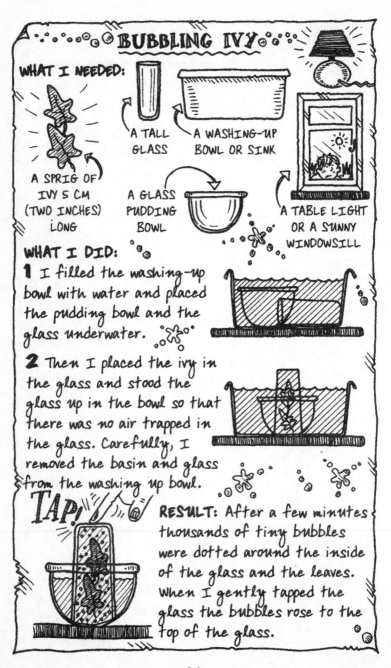

WHAT I NEEDED:

A SPRIG OF IVY 5 CM (TWO INCHES) LONG

A TALL GLASS

A WASHING-UP BOWL OR SINK

A GLASS PUDDING BOWL

A TABLE LIGHT OR A SUNNY WINDOWSILL

WHAT I DID:

1 I filled the washing-up bowl with water and placed the pudding bowl and the glass underwater.

2 Then I placed the ivy in the glass and stood the glass up in the bowl so that there was no air trapped in the glass. Carefully, I removed the basin and glass from the washing up bowl.

TAP!

RESULT: After a few minutes thousands of tiny bubbles were dotted around the inside of the glass and the leaves. When I gently tapped the glass the bubbles rose to the top of the glass.

86

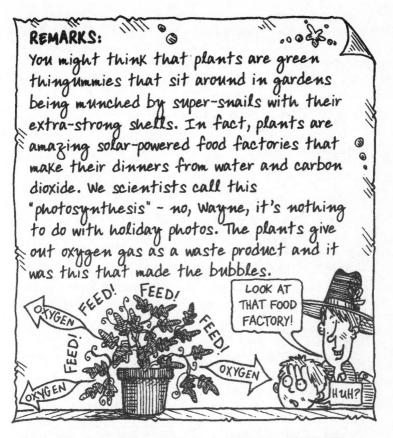

REMARKS:
You might think that plants are green thingummies that sit around in gardens being munched by super-snails with their extra-strong shells. In fact, plants are amazing solar-powered food factories that make their dinners from water and carbon dioxide. We scientists call this "photosynthesis" - no, Wayne, it's nothing to do with holiday photos. The plants give out oxygen gas as a waste product and it was this that made the bubbles.

OXYGEN FEED! FEED! FEED! OXYGEN

LOOK AT THAT FOOD FACTORY!

HUH?

Notice anything? To explain his experiments Will D Beest found himself talking about chemicals. But that's not too surprising because living things (yes, living things like your pet hamster and even primitive forms of life like your little brother/sister) are stuffed with chemicals. And so is everything else in the universe ... including the next chapter!

CURIOUS CHEMISTRY EXPERIMENTS

I expect you do chemistry experiments all the time. Like the one where you subject a block of gluten and carbohydrate to infra red radiation and discover that oxidation has resulted in partial carbonization...

Oops, sorry readers! I banged my head and started talking like a scientist! I meant to say "like when you make toast and the heat burns the bread and some of it goes black". Yes, chemicals are all around us and so are chemical changes. Chemical experiments are a much-needed attempt to make sense of all this chemical chaos.

Explosive experiments fact file

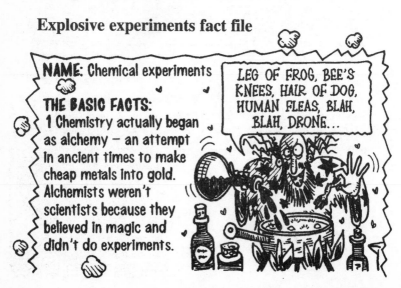

NAME: Chemical experiments

THE BASIC FACTS:
1 Chemistry actually began as alchemy – an attempt in ancient times to make cheap metals into gold. Alchemists weren't scientists because they believed in magic and didn't do experiments.

LEG OF FROG, BEE'S KNEES, HAIR OF DOG, HUMAN FLEAS, BLAH, BLAH, DRONE...

HALF AN OUNCE OF SODIUM... HEAT FOR 30 SECONDS, BLAH, BLAH...

2 The first proper chemistry experiments were performed in the 1700s when chemists began to measure their ingredients and record their results in a scientific manner.

EXPLOSIVE DETAILS: Chemistry can go wrong and blow up. For example... When polythene was invented in 1932 scientists heated the chemical ethylene in a high pressure container.

The experiment worked and the ethylene formed plastic strands that could be made into polythene sheets. But the factory blew up several times when the process went wrong. (For more explosive info, see page 135.)

IT'S A BOOM TIME FOR SCIENTIFIC EXPERIMENTS

One big chemistry breakthrough occurred in 1661 when Irish chemist Robert Boyle (1627-1691) claimed correctly that chemicals are made up of atoms or tiny clumps of atoms called molecules. And although molecules are far too small to see, one scientist found a way to prove they existed...

Horrible Science Hall of Fame: Robert Brown

(1773-1858) Nationality: Scottish

Robert Brown wasn't even a chemist, he was a botanist, and the most exciting time of his life was when he joined an expedition to explore the coast of Australia. Amazingly, he

didn't throw up with seasickness once during the entire four-year voyage. (His shipmates must have been *green* with envy). The ship leaked and eventually had to be abandoned, but Brown got a lift back to Britain in another ship. He took with him 4,000 plants he had collected and all of them were new to science.

One day, the scientist was looking at pollen grains (these are the dusty bits you get in flowers) under the microscope when he saw that something very odd was happening. Here's how he might have recorded it in his diary.

London, 1827
I can't understand it! I put some pollen in a drop of water (it makes the pollen easier to view) and the grains kept moving around. I *got* really excited because I thought that the pollen was swimming but I'm not so sure now ... you see, I tested other substances too:

MILK   INK   DYE

SNOT FROM MY NOSE.
(I'VE HAD A TERRIBLE COLD FOR MONTHS!)

They all contained little bits that danced around in the water! Why? — that's what I'd like to know!

Other scientists were fairly sure that the molecules of water were bumping into the pollen grains and making them move, but no one could prove it until science superstar Albert Einstein (1879-1955) measured the effect and worked out its mathematical basis in 1905. Could you make a great discovery like this? Here's your chance to find out as we dive into the secret experiment notebooks of super-science teacher Miss Esmerelda Perkins.

Will you be shaken or stirred?

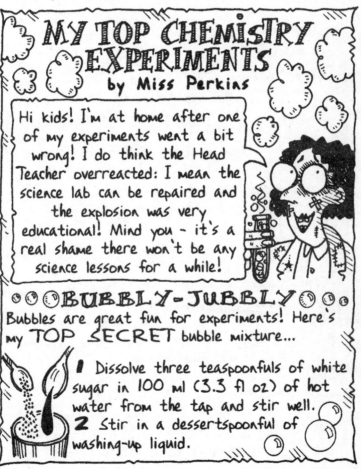

MY TOP CHEMISTRY EXPERIMENTS
by Miss Perkins

Hi kids! I'm at home after one of my experiments went a bit wrong! I do think the Head Teacher overreacted: I mean the science lab can be repaired and the explosion was very educational! Mind you - it's a real shame there won't be any science lessons for a while!

∞∞ BUBBLY-JUBBLY ∞∞

Bubbles are great fun for experiments! Here's my TOP SECRET bubble mixture...

1 Dissolve three teaspoonfuls of white sugar in 100 ml (3.3 fl oz) of hot water from the tap and stir well.

2 Stir in a dessertspoonful of washing-up liquid.

3 Stir in a tablespoonful of clear shower or hand gel. (It must contain glycerin, so check the ingredients first.)

WHAT I NEEDED:

A CYLINDRICAL CONTAINER – A SMARTIES TUBE IS IDEAL

A SHARP PENCIL

SOME SCISSORS

SOME SECRET BUBBLE MIXTURE

A PAPER HANKIE (NOT A SNOTTY ONE, PLEASE).

A RULER

SOME BLU-TAK

SOME THREAD

WHAT I DID:

1 I separated the layers of tissue paper in the hankie and cut a thin strip off one layer 2 cm (0.8 inches) wide.

2 I tied some thread to the paper and stuck the other end to a shelf with Blu-tak so that the paper was hanging from the thread.

3 I used the sharpened pencil to make a hole in the end of the container 0.5 cm (0.2 inches) wide.

4 Now for the exciting bit! I put the open end of the container in the bubble mix and stirred it around. Then I blew gently through the small hole. A big bubble appeared from the open end.

5 I put the end with the small hole close to the tissue paper...

RESULT:
The tissue paper began to wave
as if there was a breeze!

REMARKS:
A bubble is made of a thin
skin of water molecules. Air molecules can escape
though this skin and make the breeze. Well, I
guess I breezed through that experiment!

COLOURFUL CHEMICALS

Bright 'n' cheerful are the words that sprang
to mind when I made this messy mixture.
I can't wait to try it in class.

⚠ HORRIBLE MESS WARNING!

Do this experiment on newspaper or your | Grrr! |
parents might have some colourful words to say!

WHAT I NEEDED:

A STRAW

A SAUCER

SOME FOOD
COLOURS

SOME
MILK

SOME
WASHING-UP
LIQUID

WHAT I DID:

1 I filled the saucer with milk.

2 Using the straw I
added a drop of each
type of food colour to
different places in the saucer.

3 I added a drop of washing-up
liquid to the centre of the saucer
... and ... oh my goodness!

RESULT:

The colours started swirling around and mixing in weird patterns. And now here's a milk joke, kids - did you hear about the cat who won a milk-drinking contest? Yes, she won by a lap, ha ha.

⚠ HORRIBLE FAMILY WARNING!

ERK!

Don't put the mixture in the cat's saucer. The shock might put her off her supper and you'll have to eat leftover cat food!

REMARKS:

Water molecules in the milk are normally attracted to one another by surface tension. The molecules of washing-up liquid pull on the water molecules, breaking them apart, and this allows food-colouring molecules to mix with the milk. Wow, kids, aren't these molecules magic!

MYSTERY FIZZING

WHAT I NEEDED:

A BOTTLE OF LEMONADE OR FIZZY WATER

THREE GLASSES LABELLED A, B AND C

SOME COOKING OIL

SOME SUGAR

WHAT I DID:

1 I smeared the inside of glass B with a little oil and added a dessertspoonful of sugar to glass C. **2** Next I poured some lemonade into each glass.

RESULT:

• Bubbles appeared in glass A with a rush and lots of bubbles formed inside the glass.
• In glass B there was less of a rush of bubbles and far fewer appeared on the sides of the glass.
• In glass C the mixture fizzed violently and there were far more bubbles than in glass A.

REMARKS:

This experiment shows how bubbles form. The bubbles are carbon dioxide gas that was forced into the drink under pressure until it dissolved in the liquid. When I opened the bottle, the pressure was released and lemonade squirted everywhere. As the pressure was released the gas formed bubbles. The bubbles formed in microscopic hollows in the glass, but when these were covered in oil the bubbles couldn't form so easily. There were loads of little hollows between the sugar grains and that's why so many bubbles appeared. I drank all the lemonade!

BURP!

THE BROWN NAIL EXPERIMENT

WHAT I NEEDED:

KITCHEN CLEANER

10 DIRTY COPPER COINS

50 ML (1.75 FL OZ) OF VINEGAR

A GLASS

A PINCH OF SALT

A 3 CM (1.2 INCH) NAIL

A SMALL SPOON

WHAT I DID:

1 I put the coins in the glass and covered them in the vinegar. Phfaw! That vinegar gets up my nose! Then I stirred in the salt and left the mixture for 5 minutes.

2 Meanwhile I cleaned the nail with kitchen cleaner and dried it carefully.

3 Hey presto! The coins were shiny. I gave the mixture a quick stir and dropped the nail in the glass.

4 I checked the experiment half an hour later.

RESULT:

Wow! The nail had turned a dull brown!

REMARKS:

The vinegar contained acid that dissolved brown copper-based chemicals from the coins - leaving them shiny. The copper mixed with the vinegar to form a new chemical, which then settled on the nail.

FANTASTIC FROST

WHAT I NEEDED:

A MAGNIFYING GLASS

20 CM (8 INCHES) OF STRING

A 3 CM (1.2 INCHES) BALL OF PLAY-DOUGH (IDEALLY A DARK COLOUR)

A RULER

A KETTLE

96

⚠️ HORRIBLE DANGER WARNING!

Kettle steam can scald you! Keep well away from the steam and get an adult to help you with this part of the experiment, otherwise your parents could get steamed up.

WHAT I DID:

1 I stuck one end of the string in the play-dough and put it in the freezer for six hours.

2 I took the play-dough out of the freezer – it was frozen hard like rock. I tied the other end of the string to the ruler and put the ruler, string and ball back in the freezer.

3 Next I brought some water to the boil in the kettle and made myself a nice cup of tea.

4 I took the ruler, string and ball out of the freezer and brought the water to the boil again. Then holding the ruler and keeping away from the steam I passed the ball through the steam about 30 cm (12 inches) from the spout.

RESULT: The ball suddenly turned white/grey.

REMARKS:

COOL!

Where the steam had touched the ball the cold had turned the steam into droplets of water and these had frozen instantly to make frost. I could see the crystals using my magnifying glass.

So how did you get on? If you found the experiments easy you might be bubbling with confidence – but have you got what it takes to be a chemist...?

Could you be a chemist?

1 In the 1790s Thomas Wedgwood (1771-1805) pasted a mixture of water and the chemical silver nitrate on to a piece of leather. What had he come up with?

a) The world's first shammy leather for cleaning windows.

b) Photography.

c) A new kind of paint.

> **Answer: b)** Silver nitrate darkens in light and was later used to coat photographic paper. Thomas managed to get images of objects placed on the leather to appear as light shapes as the chemical around them darkened, but there was a problem: the images darkened in the light so you could only show people your photos in the dark. Modern photography became possible after scientists developed chemicals called fixatives to stop this happening.

2 In 1828 German scientist Friedrich Wöhler (1800-1882) managed to make urea. This chemical is normally found in pee – how did Wöhler make the substance?

a) He gave his baby sister a big drink and then studied the contents of her potty.

b) He heated up another chemical in a test tube.

c) He found it in school dinner soup – it turned out that the urea had come from rat pee.

Answer: b) And this is surprising because at the time scientists thought that chemicals found in living bodies could only be made by living cells. Oddly enough, Wöhler had studied urea as a medical student and performed experiments on smelly dogs' pee. He said:

...*chemistry just now is enough to drive one mad.*

Tell that to your chemistry teacher – if you dare!

3 US engineer George Goble experimented with different ways to get his barbecue burgers grilled faster. Unfortunately, one of these methods blew up the barbie. Which one?
a) Using a vacuum cleaner to blow air into the fire.
b) Using the heating fuel propane gas.
c) Covering the fuel in oxygen gas that was so cold it had turned to liquid.

HORRIBLE DANGER WARNING!
Don't try any of these. If you blow up the family barbecue (and live to tell the tale) your pocket money is sure to go up in smoke.

Dare you discover ... chemistry experiments?

Well hopefully you're burning to try some more
experiments – Miss Perkins certainly is! That's why she's
come up with an experiment quiz for you to try. (Being a
teacher she likes nothing better than to set a few questions.)

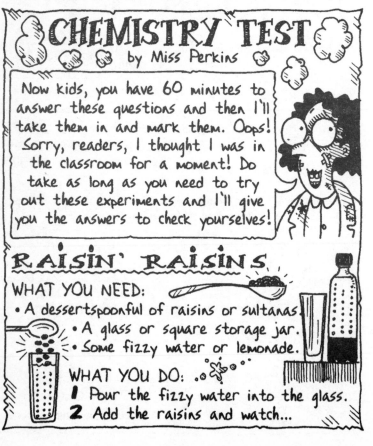

CHEMISTRY TEST
by Miss Perkins

Now kids, you have 60 minutes to
answer these questions and then I'll
take them in and mark them. Oops!
Sorry, readers, I thought I was in
the classroom for a moment! Do
take as long as you need to try
out these experiments and I'll give
you the answers to check yourselves!

RAISIN' RAISINS

WHAT YOU NEED:
• A dessertspoonful of raisins or sultanas.
• A glass or square storage jar.
• Some fizzy water or lemonade.

WHAT YOU DO:
1 Pour the fizzy water into the glass.
2 Add the raisins and watch...

What did you notice?

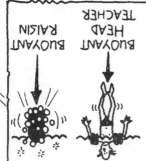

BUOYANT HEAD TEACHER

BUOYANT RAISIN

Answer: The raisins sink to the bottom, but then bubbles form in the wrinkles of the raisins and they rise to the top before sinking again. This can happen several times. The bubbles are like water wings – they make the raisins more buoyant and so they float. (Psst, I thought up this experiment after seeing the Head Teacher in the school swimming pool. He's wrinkled like a raisin and he wears water wings, hee hee!)

SCIENTIFIC NOTE

And if you want to know why bubbles are forming on the raisins, see page 95.

HOW TO SEE AIR

WHAT YOU NEED: • A radiator or heater under a window. • A sunny day. • A table. • A large piece of white paper.

WHAT YOU DO:

1 Make sure that the radiator is hot.

2 Place the paper on the table and the table close to the radiator so that the sunlight falls on the paper.

What did you notice?

Answer:

Swirling smoky patterns appear on the paper. As the air around the radiator is heated the molecules warm up and this makes them move faster. They move apart and this makes the heated air rise. Now kids, I'm sure your science teacher would want me to tell you that the correct word for this is "convection" (con-veck-shun). You're looking at shadows made by the rising air. Isn't that amazing!

COOL — I MEAN WARM!

LEMON JUICE SHOCKER

WHAT YOU NEED:
- Some lemon juice.
- A glass of warm water.
- A tea bag

WHAT YOU DO:

1 Dunk the tea bag in the glass of water. The water goes brown.

2 Add some lemon juice drop by drop to the water.

What did you notice?

Answer:

The water turns a pale yellow. The lemon juice contains acid that breaks apart the molecules in the tea and makes them paler. This chemical change is called "bleaching" – make sure you remember that word, I might test you on it later! It's a pity to waste the tea so I drank it. Yes, I do like a nice refreshing cup of lemon tea. I once made a cup for the Head Teacher but he spat it out – he was very YELL-OW! sour after that.

HIGH-TENSION EXPERIMENT

WHAT YOU NEED:
• A lump of polystyrene or a table tennis ball. • A glass of water filled to the top. • Some coins.

WHAT YOU DO:

1 Place the ball or polystyrene on the water. It will move to the side of the glass.

2 One by one slip the coins into the water (don't drop them in!) until the glass is full and the water bulges over the sides but doesn't quite spill over.

What did you notice?

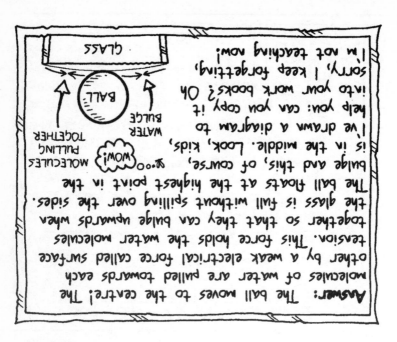

Answer: The ball moves to the centre! The molecules of water are pulled towards each other by a weak electrical force called surface tension. This force holds the water molecules together so that they can bulge upwards when the glass is full without spilling over the sides. The ball floats at the highest point in the bulge and this, of course, is in the middle. Look, kids, I've drawn a diagram to help you: can you copy it into your work books? Oh sorry, I keep forgetting, I'm not teaching now!

WATER PULLING TOGETHER

WATER BULGE

BALL

MOLECULES PULLING TOGETHER

Wow! ºo•º MOLECULES

GLASS

Explosive expressions

A scientist says:

WATER IS DISPLACED!

Do you say…?

WALTER IS DISGRACED? WHAT'S HE DONE?

Answer: Wrong! The scientist is trying to explain that the coins push water out of the way and this is why it rises upwards.

104

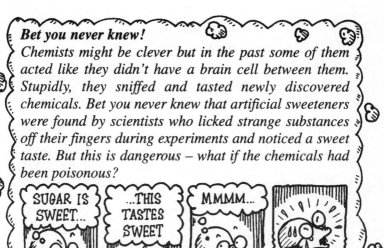

Bet you never knew!
Chemists might be clever but in the past some of them acted like they didn't have a brain cell between them. Stupidly, they sniffed and tasted newly discovered chemicals. Bet you never knew that artificial sweeteners were found by scientists who licked strange substances off their fingers during experiments and noticed a sweet taste. But this is dangerous – what if the chemicals had been poisonous?

And now for some *really* dangerous experiments...

This is the story of two scientists who were fascinated by gases and didn't mind the odd dangerous experiment or even dangerously odd experiment. Their names were John Haldane (1892-1964) and his dad John Haldane (1860-1936). (Being scientists, the Haldanes weren't too imaginative with their names.)

Here's what John senior's diary might have looked like.

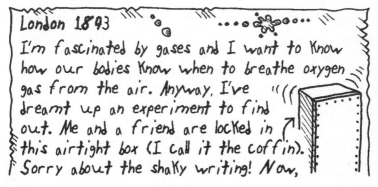

London 1893
I'm fascinated by gases and I want to know how our bodies know when to breathe oxygen gas from the air. Anyway, I've dreamt up an experiment to find out. Me and a friend are locked in this airtight box (I call it the coffin). Sorry about the shaky writing! Now,

did I remember to tell anyone where we were? We're running out of air - it must be because our bodies are using up the oxygen in the air of the box. Now we're panting. Er, I think I've had enough, I'm going to faint. If someone doesn't rescue us we'll die... Help! Gasp! Help!

(Later) Phew! We've been rescued and I've just about recovered! Still feeling tired tho'. Maybe I could do with a coffin break — I mean coffee break! Well, I've proved that when the carbon dioxide in the blood increases, this makes the body breathe faster. (Carbon dioxide is the gas that the body produces as a waste product from breathing, by the way!) I think it makes the body breathe faster to get more oxygen.

1894 ~ For my next experiment I breathed from a gas-filled football containing less oxygen than you normally get in the air. My face turned blue and my chest started heaving — it was lack of oxygen that did it. I must have looked really colourful! BLUE!

Must try this again some time!

1895 ~ Some gases kill people so I thought it was time to test them on myself. Actually I'd just got into this when I heard of how five workers died in a sewer after breathing a foul stinking gas. Anyway, I threw myself into my work (down the sewer) and found the gas was hydrogen sulphide – that's the gas they put in stink bombs. It's sometimes found in farts, and breathing too much can smother a person – so I raised a stink with the authorities about safety.

POOEY PONG!

A few months later...

I've just been testing the effects of another poison – carbon monoxide – on blood. (It stops the blood carrying oxygen.) Luckily, my lad John provided some blood to test – that's me boy! He's a chip off the old test-tube!

1903 – Me and young John are down a coalmine testing the effects of breathing firedamp – this is a mix of gases including methane (another gas found in farts). Anyway, I've just told young John to take a deep breath and read out a speech from Shakespeare... Oops, he's panting, he's gasping, he's fallen over in a faint – it looks like he's suffering from lack of oxygen. Yes, yes, YES – that's what I call a successful result!

FRIENDS, ROMANS, COUNTRYMEN...

Now, *you're* not silly enough to try any of these are you?

Oddly enough, young John really *enjoyed* the experiments. Well, it was better than going to his brutal school where he was bullied just because he was clever. And when he was 15, young John began his own experiments on his sister's guinea pigs. He bred over 300 animals and proved that pairs of genes, such as those for certain colours and curly hair, go together.

John Junior became a scientist and enjoyed dangerous underwater experiments on submarine safety. When he died he left his body to science ... to be used for medical experiments.

What's that? You don't like the thought of performing science experiments on dead bodies? Oh dear. The scientists in the next chapter really would like a dead body for a test, but I'm sure they could dig one up somewhere. Why not *crash* through to the next page and find out what they're up to...?

FRANTIC FORCES EXPERIMENTS

It's an odd thought ... but scientists have worked out the scientific and mathematical basis for every move you're likely to make in your whole life! They even know what would happen if you went to the moon in a rocket. And it's all down to the science of forces!

Explosive experiments fact file

NAME: Forces experiments

THE BASIC FACTS: 1 A force makes an object move or alter course. Examples might include gravity making a brick fall on your head or an alert friend pushing you out of the way just in time.

BRICK

ALERT FRIEND

HELLO AGAIN!

2 The first person to experiment in a scientific way with forces was our old pal Galileo. Remember what he was up to on page 15?

3 He invented experiments designed to show that objects of the same size fall at the same speed no matter how heavy they are. Galileo rolled balls of different weights down ramps and found that they always moved at the same speed.

GOOD, EH?

4 Superstar scientist Isaac Newton (1642-1727) put Galileo's ideas and other basic principles of forces on a mathematical basis in his book, the *Principia* (1687).

EXPLOSIVE DETAILS: I don't want to worry you, but some forces experiments involve car crashes and jumping out of balloons hundreds of metres above the ground.

Oh, so you're not too worried about the danger and you want to try some frantic forces experiments yourself?

OK, feel free to try these tests from the notebook of Professor N Large, accident-prone inventor and scientist. Any footprints and fluff you might notice belong to his cat, Tiddles.

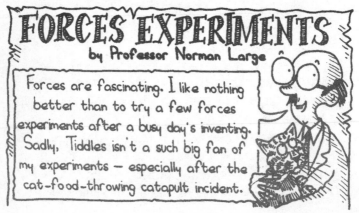

FORCES EXPERIMENTS
by Professor Norman Large

Forces are fascinating. I like nothing better than to try a few forces experiments after a busy day's inventing. Sadly, Tiddles isn't a such big fan of my experiments — especially after the cat-food-throwing catapult incident.

TREMENDOUS TYRES

You may not know this but rubber tyres were invented by a Scot, Robert Thomson (1822-1873), who believed that rubber tyres would help carts to travel more quickly. And in 1847 he proved it using an experiment. Here's my version of Thomson's test.

WHAT I NEEDED:

ANY TOY CAR OR LORRY WITH LARGE TYRES THAT YOU CAN REMOVE

A TOY BUCKET

SOME SCALES

SOME BLU-TAK

SOME BOOKS

A PROTRACTOR

SOME STRING

SOME CORRUGATED CARDBOARD

A MEASURING JUG

A TABLE

WHAT I DID:

1 I propped one end of the table up by putting books under the feet of the table. The angle of the slope was 10°.

2 Then I stuck the cardboard to the tabletop with Blu-tak. Tiddles, get off that table!

3 I used the string to tie the handle of the bucket to the front axle of the car.

4 I measured 50 ml (1.75 fl oz) of water into the jug and poured it into the bucket.

CORRUGATED CARDBOARD

LAZY CAT

LORRY

BOOKS

PROTRACTOR

10°

TOY BUCKET

111

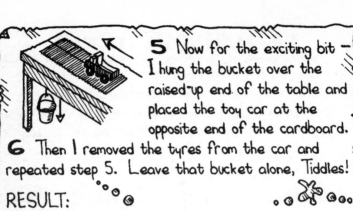

5 Now for the exciting bit — I hung the bucket over the raised-up end of the table and placed the toy car at the opposite end of the cardboard.

6 Then I removed the tyres from the car and repeated step 5. Leave that bucket alone, Tiddles!

RESULT:

The car was pulled forward by the weight of the water in the bucket. But when the tyres were removed the car couldn't move easily over the bumps. Also, Tiddles got soaked when she knocked the bucket over.

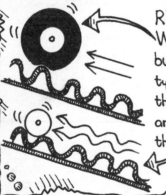

REMARKS:

When rubber tyres go over bumps they squash up. Without tyres the wheels had to lift the whole car over the bumps and this took more force so the vehicle moved more slowly.

This is what Thomson's experiment showed too.

Bet you never knew!
A shortage of rubber meant that Thomson's idea didn't catch on, but when rubber became more widely available in 1888 the idea was reinvented by John Boyd Dunlop (1840-1921). He got the idea after his son got a sore bum pedalling around on an iron-wheeled tricycle.

Now back to N Large's notebook.

CURIOUS CARD

WHAT I NEEDED:

A PIECE OF CARD   A RULER   A DRAWING PIN   SOME SCISSORS   A COTTON REEL

WHAT I DID:

1 I cut out a piece of card 3 cm (1.2 inches) across.

2 I stuck the drawing pin in the middle of the card and placed it upside-down so that the point of the pin stuck upwards. Careful now, Tiddles — it's sharp!

3 Finally I placed the cotton reel over the point and on top of the card. I took a deep breath and blew down the hole while gently lifting the reel.

BLOW!

RESULT:

You might think that the air will blow the card downwards — but the pin and the card actually rose up with the reel. Well, it did until Tiddles knocked it with her paw and it fell off. Yes, Tiddles, I'll give you your supper in a moment!

HURRY UP!

REMARKS:

The air from my breath passed through the reel and spread over the card. Because the air in my breath

was moving faster than the air under the card, it was pressing less hard (we scientists call this force air pressure). This allowed the air under the card to lift it up. This sounds a little complicated but hopefully my diagram will explain things better!

BREATH

AIR PRESSURE

THE AMAZING BUCKET EXPERIMENT

HORRIBLE MESS WARNING!

This experiment is best done outside!

WHAT I NEEDED:

A VOLUNTEER TO SIT (OR LIE) ON THE GROUND. STAY PUT, TIDDLES.

A CHAIR TO STAND ON

A TOY BUCKET WITH 40 cm (ABOUT 16 INCHES) OF STRING TIED TO THE HANDLE.

A RUBBER OR LEATHER GLOVE.

WHAT I DID:

1 I put on the glove to protect my hand during the experiment and filled the bucket one-third full of water.

2 I stood on the chair and made sure there was enough room to swing the bucket round on the string without knocking the volunteer, who was busy lapping her milk.

THERE'S ENOUGH ROOM TO SWING A CAT—I MEAN BUCKET

114

3 I swung the bucket around on the string.

RESULT:

No water came out even when the bucket was upside-down. At this point the whirling bucket whacked into me and I got soaked but this time Tiddles escaped by a whisker.

REMARKS:

As it went around in a circle the water kept trying to fly off in a straight line. (We scientists call this effect "centrifugal force.") The sides of the bucket stopped the water escaping and centrifugal force prevented the water from falling down under the influence of gravity.

CENTRIFUGAL FORCE

THE IMPOSSIBLE BAG TEST

WHAT I NEEDED:

AN EMPTY SWING BIN (NOTE: IT'S QUITE ALL RIGHT TO USE A NEW PEDAL-BIN BAG AND AN EMPTY PEDAL-BIN.)

A NEW SWING BIN LINER

WHAT I DID:

1 I placed the bag inside the bin with its edges hanging outside below the rim of the bin.

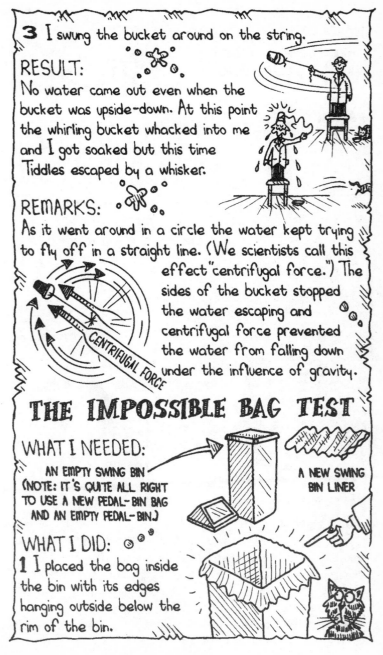

115

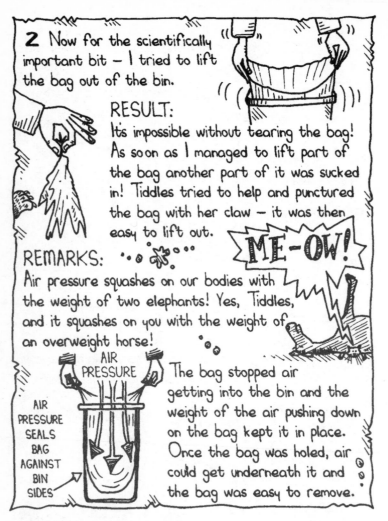

2 Now for the scientifically important bit — I tried to lift the bag out of the bin.

RESULT:
It's impossible without tearing the bag! As soon as I managed to lift part of the bag another part of it was sucked in! Tiddles tried to help and punctured the bag with her claw — it was then easy to lift out.

ME-OW!

REMARKS:
Air pressure squashes on our bodies with the weight of two elephants! Yes, Tiddles, and it squashes on you with the weight of an overweight horse!

AIR PRESSURE

AIR PRESSURE SEALS BAG AGAINST BIN SIDES

The bag stopped air getting into the bin and the weight of the air pushing down on the bag kept it in place. Once the bag was holed, air could get underneath it and the bag was easy to remove.

Four famous forces feats

1 In 1640 French scientist Pierre Gassendi (1592-1655) wanted to find out what happened if you dropped a ball from a moving vehicle. Did the ball fly forward in the air or backwards, for example? So he climbed up the mast of a slave galley. The slaves were chained to their oars for years and had to poo where they sat, so the stink was appalling. But the forceful Frenchman dropped a series of balls and found that they fell straight down. In other words the balls were falling forward with the motion of the ship.

2 Scientist Benjamin Robbins (1707-1751) worked out that you could measure the speed of an object by crashing it into a heavy pendulum. The faster the object's speed the further the pendulum moved. So here's an experiment idea – pedal your bike as fast as you can down a steep slope and slam into a punch bag and see how high it swings. On second thoughts, maybe your science teacher would be interested in trying this experiment? You could even set it up as a surprise for when he arrives at school on his bicycle...

3 The forces behind flying golf balls were worked out by golf-crazy Scottish scientist Peter Guthrie Tait (1831-1901). Guthrie spent nine years performing experiments which involved hitting golf balls with a golf club. Then he relaxed by playing golf.

He worked out that the ball always fell in a low arc and was lifted in the air by its spin.

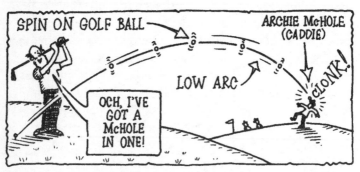

Tait then got hate mail from other golfers who reckoned he was trying to cheat.

4 In the 1870s a Belgian named de Groof invented a parachute made of silk and cane and controlled by levers. He experimented to see how it worked by jumping out of balloons. (In fact, parachutes trap air under the falling canopy and this slows the fall.) The tests involved some hard moments – like when de Groof hit the ground, for example.

AIR TRAPPED HERE   AIR TRAPPED HERE

IT'S AN 'AIR-RAISING EXPERIENCE!

De Groof's final downfall happened when his parachute fell to bits high above the River Thames. Poor De Groof – he threw himself into his work but made a larger splash than he intended.

Could you be a forces scientist?

1 In 1848 London was full of ghostly rumours. The latest fashion was for seances in which a circle of people pressed fingers on a table and thought hard. It was widely believed that ghosts passed on messages by tipping over the tables. What happened when Michael Faraday set up an experiment to test these claims?

a) A headless ghost appeared and chased the scientist away.

b) The experiment proved that table-tipping was caused by the twitching of tired fingers.

c) The scientist found out that the seance organizers were crooks who had tied string to the tables.

TONIGHT 100% genuine SEANCE (NO STRINGS ATTACHED)

2 In 1909 a Major Hardcastle wanted to find out what happened to bullets fired in the air. So he sat on a boat on a river and blazed away at the sky with his rifle. His butler had to collect bullets that fell on the shore protected only by a thick book on top of his head.

How did this experiment end?

a) A bullet hit a flying duck. The dead duck fell from the sky and brained the butler.

b) A falling bullet mashed the major.

c) No one got shot because the bullets didn't fall down in a straight line.

Dare you discover ... forces?

So do you reckon you could be a fantastic forces scientist? Well, if you can find out the results of these frantic experiments set for you by Professor Large then you'll be a force to be reckoned with.

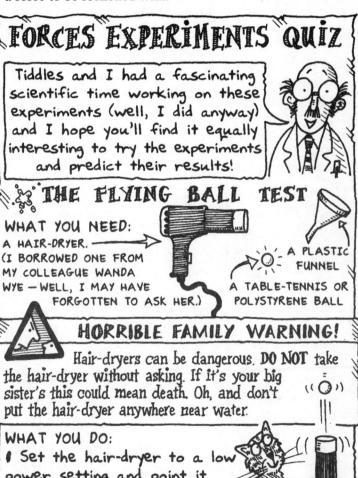

FORCES EXPERIMENTS QUIZ

Tiddles and I had a fascinating scientific time working on these experiments (well, I did anyway) and I hope you'll find it equally interesting to try the experiments and predict their results!

THE FLYING BALL TEST

WHAT YOU NEED:

A HAIR-DRYER.
(I BORROWED ONE FROM MY COLLEAGUE WANDA WYE — WELL, I MAY HAVE FORGOTTEN TO ASK HER.)

A PLASTIC FUNNEL

A TABLE-TENNIS OR POLYSTYRENE BALL

HORRIBLE FAMILY WARNING!

Hair-dryers can be dangerous. DO NOT take the hair-dryer without asking. If it's your big sister's this could mean death. Oh, and don't put the hair-dryer anywhere near water.

WHAT YOU DO:

1 Set the hair-dryer to a low power setting and point it upwards. Place the ball in the stream of air. The ball floats. Tiddles! Leave that ball alone!

121

2 Now place the ball in the funnel and blow air up the spout.

What did you notice?

BLOW!

AIR PRESSURE

DON'T TOUCH THE FUNNEL WITH THE HAIR-DRYER.

Answer: Look, Tiddles - the ball doesn't rise up! In the first case the force of the air pushing up from the hair-dryer was enough to support the weight of the ball. The funnel, however, makes the air rush around the ball rather than pushing the ball upwards. The slower-moving air above the ball presses it downwards, trapping it in the funnel. I have drawn a diagram to show the forces involved.

°AIR-POWER EXPERIMENT

WHAT YOU NEED:

TWO GLASSES ➞

A BATH OR WASHING UP BOWL OF WATER. (I HAD TO DO THE WASHING UP BEFORE I COULD START THIS EXPERIMENT.)

WHAT YOU DO:

1 Hold one glass under water and turn it upside-down. Then lift up the glass so that the rim is almost clear of the water. The glass is still full of water because air pressing down on the water outside the glass pushes the water upwards inside the glass. Hmm, time for another diagram I think.

2 Put the second glass into the water upside-down so that air is trapped inside it.

3 Carefully move the second glass so that it's just beneath the water-filled glass and slowly turn it the right way up. An air bubble should rise up into the water-filled glass.

AIR PRESSURE AIR PRESSURE

WATER PUSHED UPWARDS

AIR BUBBLE

What did you notice?

Answer: The water-filled glass empties! The force of the air pushes the water out. Yes, this experiment is a real wash-out – sorry, that was meant to be a joke!

EMPTY GLASS

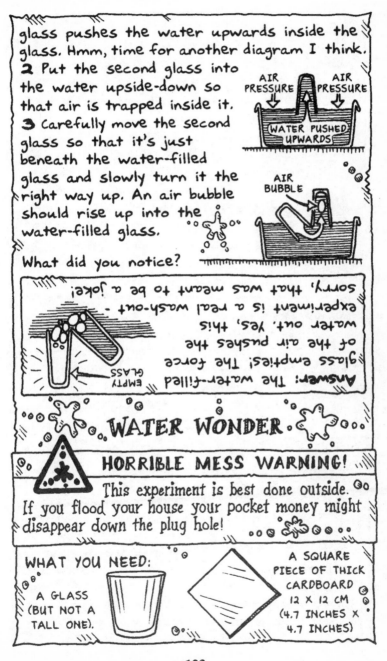

WATER WONDER

HORRIBLE MESS WARNING!

This experiment is best done outside. If you flood your house your pocket money might disappear down the plug hole!

WHAT YOU NEED:

A GLASS (BUT NOT A TALL ONE).

A SQUARE PIECE OF THICK CARDBOARD 12 X 12 CM (4.7 INCHES X 4.7 INCHES)

WHAT YOU DO:

1 Fill the glass so full of water that the water bulges over at the brim.

2 Gently push the cardboard down over the glass - try to make sure there are no bubbles and no water gets spilt.

OOER!

3 Carefully turn the glass and the cardboard upside-down. You should be holding the glass with one hand and supporting the cardboard with the other. Once again you need to make sure that there are no bubbles and no water gets spilt.

4 OK - are you ready for this? Remove the hand supporting the cardboard... Yes, you did read that right. Well, get on with it! Everything's going to be fine ...

HORRIBLE DIFFICULTY WARNING!

You might need to practise this experiment once or twice to get it right. But don't practise this experiment with your brother or sister underneath.

What did you notice?

AIR PRESSURE

WOW!

Answer: The cardboard stays in place and the water remains in the glass! Since there is no air in the glass to push against the cardboard from above, the air pressure pushing up against the cardboard is strong enough to keep the cardboard pressed upwards against the rim of the glass.

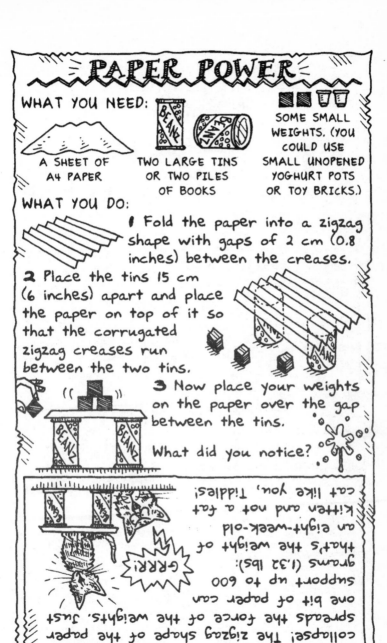

PAPER POWER

WHAT YOU NEED:

A SHEET OF A4 PAPER

TWO LARGE TINS OR TWO PILES OF BOOKS

SOME SMALL WEIGHTS. (YOU COULD USE SMALL UNOPENED YOGHURT POTS OR TOY BRICKS.)

WHAT YOU DO:

1 Fold the paper into a zigzag shape with gaps of 2 cm (0.8 inches) between the creases.

2 Place the tins 15 cm (6 inches) apart and place the paper on top of it so that the corrugated zigzag creases run between the two tins.

3 Now place your weights on the paper over the gap between the tins.

What did you notice?

Answer: Amazingly, the paper doesn't collapse! The zigzag shape of the paper spreads the force of the weights. Just one bit of paper can support up to 600 grams (1.32 lbs): that's the weight of an eight-week-old kitten and not a fat cat like you, Tiddles!

GRRR!

125

BODY BALANCE TEST

WHAT YOU NEED:

YOUR OWN BODY   A WALL   A COIN   A RULER

WHAT YOU DO:

1 Place the coin on the floor 70 cm (28 inches) from the wall.

2 Stand with your back to the wall and your heels touching the skirting-board.

3 Try to bend over and pick up the coin without your heels losing touch with the wall. (You're not allowed to crouch down either.)

WALL

COIN

70CM

NGHH!

What did you notice?

Answer: It's really hard! Your every move has to be balanced in terms of gravity. So when you bend you have to stick out your, er - what can I call it? Ah yes, your back-side to balance the force pulling on your upper body as you bend.

126

With the wall in the way you can't do this - so it's almost impossible to pick up the coin without falling forward. I asked Wanda Wye to try but I'm afraid she had to back out.

I WONDERED WHY - ARGH! NOW I KNOW!

And talking about forces and bodies – did you know that some experiments involve both forces and bodies? Yes, we're talking about crash testing – and you're about to go on a crash course in these extreme experiments with the man who dreamt up the idea.

He was no crash test dummy...

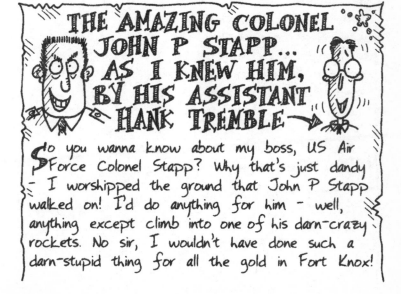

THE AMAZING COLONEL JOHN P STAPP... AS I KNEW HIM, BY HIS ASSISTANT HANK TREMBLE

So you wanna know about my boss, US Air Force Colonel Stapp? Why that's just dandy - I worshipped the ground that John P Stapp walked on! I'd do anything for him - well, anything except climb into one of his darn-crazy rockets. No sir, I wouldn't have done such a darn-stupid thing for all the gold in Fort Knox!

127

I first met the Colonel back in 1955. Well, straight up I knew he was a special kinda fella. He wasn't much to look at - a plump guy with a squarish forehead, a crew cut, big sticking-out ears and a permanent goofy grin. But heck - was he brave!

"Tremble," he said, "I just gotta try these dangerous tests. I owe it to them boys who fly our jets to find out the effects of using an ejector seat so we can make them planes as safe as possible." What a guy!

So the Colonel and a few darn-crazy volunteers took it in turns to sit in this swing-chair machine and get smashed against a pole. The Colonel asked me if I wanted a swing - but I saw what happened to the guys who got hurt so I passed on that one. Not that the Colonel minded. No, sir! His mind was fixed on something far more dangerous...

It was a kind of metal box on rails and powered by rockets - the Colonel called it "Gee-Whizz". His plan was to fire the rockets and crash the box into a set of buffers at six hundred miles an hour - with him on board! I'll never forget that first experiment.

"Say, Tremble, you wanna ride with me? It'll feel just like a real plane crash!" said the Colonel.

I knew that twinkle in his eye so I forced a smile. "No, Colonel Stapp, sir - I'll think I'll watch!"

"As you wish," replied the Colonel.

"Is that thing safe, sir?" I stammered.
"Well, there's sure as heck just one way to find out!" said the Colonel, swinging himself into the cockpit. His mechanics strapped him into his seat and handed him his shiny crash helmet. A doctor checked Colonel Stapp's blood pressure and, though I didn't like to say nothing, I figured he was a goner.

With a roar, the engines fired up and a cloud of smoke enveloped the box - then I saw it scooting along the track like a missile. I couldn't look so I screwed up my eyes and heard the crash. In a split second the sound went though my body like a shock wave. I imagined the Colonel's body - it wasn't a pretty sight. I didn't dare open my eyes, but I took off my hat as a mark of respect.

That day the Colonel became the fastest man in the world. I saw him afterwards being removed from the metal box. He was still alive but his eyes were bleeding! There were bruises and cuts all over his body - and he wasn't grinning no more. So I figured he'd give up experimenting but I was wrong.

"I'll be back tomorrow," the Colonel croaked.

And he was. In all, the Colonel put himself through that ordeal 26 times.

That man was a living legend!

Next, the Colonel got the notion of using dummies

26

for testing. So he had an artificial-leg designer make a dummy. It was the world's first crash test dummy. He wanted to check out what happens to pilots who fall from planes — so he had dummies dropped from aircraft. Everything went just fine until them pesky dummies plunged into a drive-in movie theatre. It darn near enough scared the pants off the audience.

Bet you never knew!

1 The Colonel was sacked after testing live pigs in car crashes. (I bet they were in need of "oinkment" for their injuries.) No one was bothered about the poor pigs, but there were complaints from car makers who didn't like anyone highlighting the dangers of their vehicles. But the Colonel was right, and by 1966 all new American cars had to be crash-tested — by law.

2 Another brave crash experimenter was US Professor Larry Patrick. He volunteered for tests such as being strapped to a vehicle and smashed into a wall. Despite feeling like his chest was being bashed with a sledge-hammer, he repeated the tests six times a day. At the Professor's retirement party everyone watched a jolly film of the tests entitled "Crazy Larry Rides Again".

PHWOAR! WOW! COOL!

I'VE HAD A SMASHING CAREER!

Crash test dummies are full of complicated measuring equipment and cost over $100,000. But if you want your own crash test programme and you can't afford $100,000, cheer up, there's a cheaper method. You're not going to believe this – but scientists have used actual dead bodies as crash test dummies!

Read on for the grisly details...

CRASH TEST
◆MAGAZINE◆

HOW TO MAKE YOUR OWN CRASH TEST DUMMY FROM A DEAD BODY

Readers have been writing in for advice on how to use dead bodies for crash testing. Well folks, here's all the info you need!

STEP 1: PREPARING THE BODY

Dead bodies go stiff after a few hours so you need a recently dead body – but do make sure it's *actually* dead first. Beware of angry relatives and vicars, etc who might be unhappy about you testing the mortal remains of dear old Uncle Bert.

TESTING TIP: If the body turns out to be stiff, it's a good idea to exercise the limbs to make them supple so that they fit in the car.

STEP 2: WOUNDS
Dead bodies don't bruise and this is a pity because you'll want to create

131

realistic crash wounds. Why not inject a special dye into the heart – this will flow through the blood vessels even though the heart is no longer pumping and leave bruise-like marks where the body gets damaged in the crash.

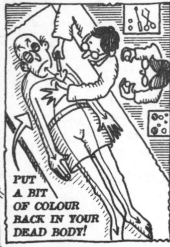

PUT A BIT OF COLOUR BACK IN YOUR DEAD BODY!

STEP 3: CHECKING THE BONES

You'll want to know about the forces affecting the bones in the crash. The best way to do this is to slice open the body and strap recording instruments to the bones.

TESTING TIP: Don't forget to sew up the body and dress it in some clothes. That way it will look nice and smart for its big day.

DEAD SMART!

STEP 4: USING YOUR BRAIN

Want to find out what happens to the head during a crash? Well, you'd best use your brain! You need to cut off the head from the body and stick a probe inside the brain to measure how it sloshes about during the crash. Then sew the head back on the body - the right way round!

RIGHT   WRONG

TESTING TIP: If you've got loads of money to spare you could use a high-speed X-ray machine.

THE BRAIN IS SLAMMED FORWARD INSIDE THE SKULL

It might not sound very nice but there's plenty of advantages in using dead bodies:

• The tests show us how crashes affect the human body.
• This data helps us to design realistic dummies and safety features such as air bags and collapsing steering-wheels designed to soak up the force of a crash.

SPOT THE DUMMY

• Dead bodies cost nothing and they don't complain.

Bet you never knew!
In 2000, an Australian car-maker developed a crash test kangaroo dummy called "Robo-roo" to show what happens when a car hits a kangaroo. This is a common accident in Australia. (If the dummy hadn't worked the scientists would have been hopping mad.)

So you've survived all those crashes? Ready for something even *more* dangerous, something even *louder*? Well, you can find it in the next explosive chapter. It's sure to go with a BANG!

133

EXPERIMENTS WITH BLASTS AND BANGS

This chapter is about explosions and noise. And I bet you'll be pleased to hear that we're going to be letting off explosives. Yes, we're going to blow up this lovely, little school.

I'm sure that when the pupils find out that their school is going to be destroyed they'll be deeply upset.

But it's all in a good cause because it will allow us to see the effects of explosives and to introduce the experiments in this chapter. But before we get to the noisy bits there's just time for a few facts.

Explosive experiments fact file

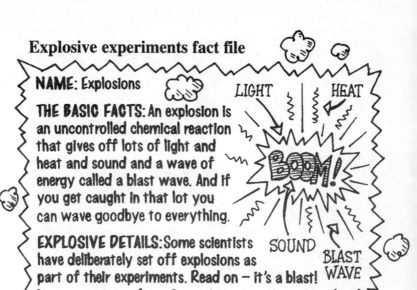

NAME: Explosions

THE BASIC FACTS: An explosion is an uncontrolled chemical reaction that gives off lots of light and heat and sound and a wave of energy called a blast wave. And if you get caught in that lot you can wave goodbye to everything.

EXPLOSIVE DETAILS: Some scientists have deliberately set off explosions as part of their experiments. Read on – it's a blast!

LIGHT HEAT

BOOM!

SOUND BLAST WAVE

Bet you never knew!
In the USA in 1880 barmy boffin Daniel Ruggles tried to cause thunderstorms by blowing up clouds.

THUNDERCLOUD

HIGH-FLYING BALLOON

ELECTRIC CABLE CARRIED SPARK TO EXPLOSIVES

CONTAINER FULL OF EXPLOSIVES

RUGGLES

THE EXPERIMENT

BANG!

In fact, the blast had no effect on the cloud because it would have rained anyway. Ruggles was just another drippy scientist with a soggy idea.

And talking about explosions, one of the most famous scientists in this department was a rather miserable Swede.

No, sorry – I meant a Swedish person who happened to have a gloomy personality and we're just about to meet him even though he's been dead for years. Yes, we've dug up Alfred Nobel for a final farewell interview.

Dead brainy: Alfred Nobel (1833-1896)

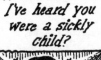

I've heard you were a sickly child?

Yes, but I've felt a lot worse since I've been dead.

And your inventor dad lost all his money...

Yes, he invented explosive bombs but he blew his chances of riches.

When you grew up you helped your brother and dad make the explosive called nitroglycerine.

I hit on the idea of using mercury fulminate – the bang used in crackers to make the explosives blow up.

BANG!

Was it dangerous?

Yes, I must have been crackers.

In 1864 your factory blew up. Your brother was killed and your dad had a fit that left him crippled. How did you feel?

It was a terrible blow!

Two years later your new factory blew up.

My hopes were blasted!

You tried countless experiments to make a safe explosive, adding stuff like sawdust to nitroglycerine.

I knew it wooden work.

At last you tried mixing the explosive with kieselguhr, a substance made from tiny crushed water-creatures. And that did work.

Yes, we had a big blow-out to celebrate!

You carried on experimenting and in 1875 you invented blasting gelatine after cutting your hand.

Yes, I put some collodion germ-killer on the wound and came up with the idea of mixing collodion and explosives to make a more powerful blast.

COLLODION + EXPLOSIVES = BIG BANG

So collodion burns easily...

Yes, I've got some here. If I could just demonstrate it...

BOOM!

WHOOPS!

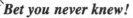

Bet you never knew!

Good stuff, collodion. Did you know that the inventor of a type of plastic called celluloid got the idea from collodion? US inventor John Wesley Hyatt (1837-1920) cut his finger and found his collodion had spilt and made a gungy mess. This inspired him to mix in other substances and make celluloid. Although the new plastic could be made into billiard balls, films, buttons and false teeth, it was explosive when heated. This meant some people suffered exploding false teeth and got a bit hot under the collar – especially since their collars were made of celluloid too.

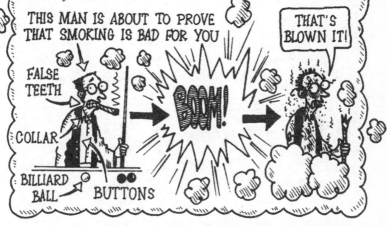

THIS MAN IS ABOUT TO PROVE THAT SMOKING IS BAD FOR YOU

THAT'S BLOWN IT!

FALSE TEETH

COLLAR

BILLIARD BALL

BUTTONS

BOOM!

Mind you, that little party popper is nothing compared to the explosion on the next page – it'll blow you away!

Yes, that school's just about ready to blow...

It's show time!

WE'VE DRILLED HOLES IN THE PILLARS HOLDING UP THE SCHOOL AND FILLED THEM WITH STICKS OF DYNAMITE

LOVELY LITTLE SCHOOL

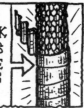

THEN WE'VE WRAPPED THE PILLARS IN CHICKEN WIRE AND TOUGH FABRIC TO SOAK UP THE FORCE OF THE BLAST. THIS MAKES SURE THAT THE EXPLOSION DESTROYS THE PILLARS BUT WON'T HURL LITTLE BITS OF SCHOOL OVER THE SURROUNDING HOUSES.

We've checked the school to make sure that there are no children inside and cleared everyone out of the houses. Oops – let's not forget the school cat, the junior class hamster and the stick insects. Well, I guess it's time to let off the explosives.

10, 9, 8, 7...

Oh, yeah – I suppose someone ought to tell the teachers to get out too...

6, 5, 4, 3, 2, 1...

BLAST!

Whilst we're waiting for the smoke to clear and the dust to settle, here's an explosive quiz.

Explosive experiments quiz

All the questions have just three possible answers:

a) The scientist was blown up.

b) The scientist lived but his lab got blown up.

c) There was an explosion but it did little damage.

1 In 1500, Chinese scientist Wan Hu attempted a brave but crazy experiment. He decided to invent manned rocket-flight – so he tied 47 rockets to the back of his chair, sat back and lit the fuse. What happened?

2 Inventor Thomas Edison (1847-1931) experimented with a helicopter powered by explosives – I suppose he wanted to move up in the world. What was the result?

3 In the 1990s scientist Steve Sparks (no, I didn't make up these names) tried an experiment to show how volcanoes explode. So did Sparks fly?

4 If you heat up liquid nitrogen (that's a gas that has been cooled until it's a liquid) it turns back into a gas with explosive force. US scientist Mark Leather wanted to use this power to launch a water container into space. What happened next?

Answers: 1 a) The chair exploded and the scientist wasn't in Wan piece when he landed. Yes, if the rocket had flown the scientist might have been thrilled to bits – instead of being in bits.

HU DOES THIS BELONG TO?

2 b) A spark blew up the machine and with it Edison's lab.
3 c) The scientist created a mix of acetone and pine resin and heated it up to show conditions inside an exploding volcano. The acetone turned into gas that formed bubbles in the resin and when they reached the surface the whole thing blew up.
4 c) The container rose a few metres and crashed to earth.

So now the dust has settled from our school explosion, let's take a look at what's left. Is the school still standing, I wonder?

As planned, the explosives broke up the columns that held up the school. The building collapsed in a heap of ruins but didn't fly apart as it would have done in an uncontrolled blast. That's what I call a *smashing* success!

Now I expect you're fired up to try some explosive experiments yourself. (Just leave the dynamite behind when you go to school.) So here's a rare peep at the notebook of scientist Wanda Wye, complete with her experiments.

Oh yeah – feel free to try them yourself!

ENERGY EXPERIMENTS
by Wanda Wye

My research includes the effects of uncontrolled exothermic reactions and the molecular effects of thermal energy.

Sorry, readers, here's an English translation: Wanda says she's interested in the effects of explosions and how heat affects different substances.

UNDERWATER VOLCANO

Volcanoes smoke because hot air rising from their craters wafts dust and ash upwards. This fascinating convection effect also happens with underwater volcanoes.

WHAT I NEEDED:

SOME PARCEL TAPE AND SCISSORS

A KETTLE

A LARGE GLASS BOWL

SOME FOOD COLOURING

A SMALL PLASTIC SHAMPOO BOTTLE (15 TO 60 ML OR 0.5 TO 2 FL OZ)

A LARGE PEBBLE OR LARGE PIECE OF PLASTICINE OR MODELLING CLAY

CONTINUED ➡

WHAT I DID:

1 I filled the large bowl with cold water.

2 I taped the small bottle to the pebble. (If I was a little more artistic I could have made a volcano model out of modelling clay and shaped it around the bottle.)

3 I boiled some water in a kettle and left it to cool for two minutes.

4 I added two drops of food colouring to the small bottle and then some hot water from the kettle until it was full to the brim.

HORRIBLE DANGER WARNING!

The water is still very hot, so get an adult to help here. (If the adult scalds themselves you can always tell them off for not feeling the water before they touched it!)

5 Nearly ready now! I placed the small bottle in the large bowl of water and sat back to enjoy the show! **AMAZING!**

RESULT: The hot coloured water rose up like the cloud of an underwater volcano. It formed spirals and clouds in the cooler water and then spread across the surface.

Over the next ten minutes the coloured water began to drop downwards. Hmm, fascinating...

> **REMARKS:** The molecules of hot water had more heat energy and this made them move apart. In this way the hot water was less dense than cold water — so it moved upwards.

Explosive expressions

A scientist says:

Do you say...?

YOU'RE DENSER THAN WATER

DUH-DENSE-WHO ME?

Answer: NO, he said you're denser than "water", not *Walter*. A substance is dense when it's heavy in relation to its size. Your body is slightly denser than the same volume of water and that's why you're mostly underwater when you swim. Air in your lungs and guts makes you more buoyant so you float.

ROCKET POPPER

I've always fancied myself as a rocket scientist and this experiment showed me how a rocket works.

HORRIBLE MESS WARNING!

This experiment is appallingly messy. Do it outside or you'll face a messy fate when your parents spot the damage.

CONTINUED

145

WHAT I NEEDED:

A FILM CONTAINER

A FUNNEL

SOME WATER IN A JUG

TWO ALKA-SELTZERS OR DENTURE CLEANING TABLETS.
(I USED THE LAST TWO ALKA-SELTZERS IN THE LAB, WHICH WAS A BIT OF A MISTAKE BECAUSE THE PROFESSOR HAD AN UPSET TUMMY THE FOLLOWING MORNING.)

A SAUCER

A ROLLING PIN

WHAT I DID:

1 I broke the tablets into bits on the saucer and used the end of the rolling pin to break the bits into smaller pieces.

CRUNCH!

2 I put the funnel into the container and poured the bits of tablets through the funnel and into the container.

3 Now for the exciting bit! I added enough water to fill the container by one third and quickly jammed on the lid and placed it upside-down on a table. Just then Tiddles, the Professor's cat, jumped on the table. Tiddles, go away!

MEEOW!

BLAST

RESULT: WOW! The container blasted off like a rocket and Tiddles raced off like a rocket. When she returned I had to brush bits of alka-seltzer off her fur before the Professor saw her.

REMARKS: A rocket flies because exploding fuel blasts out behind it. The backward blast actually pushes the rocket forward! My rocket was powered by a chemical reaction. The water mixing with the pills made carbon dioxide gas and a fast-growing bubble of gas forced open the top and blew the container up in the air.

FORCE!

THE SURPRISING BALLOON EXPERIMENT

WHAT I NEEDED:

A BALLOON

A PIN

A PIECE OF STICKY TAPE ROUGHLY 12 CM X 1.75 CM (4.75 INCHES X 0.6 INCHES)

WHAT I DID:

1 I blew up the balloon and knotted the end.

2 I stuck the tape on the balloon.

3 Now for the exciting bit – I slowly stuck the pin through the tape. The Professor and Tiddles dived for cover...

ARGH!

147

CONTINUED →

RESULT: Nothing much happened. The air began to escape from the hole made by the pin but there was NO EXPLOSION.

REMARKS: When you blow up a balloon the rubber stretches and so stores the energy of this force. Normally balloons burst because the energy is suddenly released, tearing the rubber. The sticky tape stopped the rubber from tearing and so the balloon couldn't burst.

By the way, did you notice how *quiet* that experiment was?

Normally, when balloons burst or things explode (like the school on page 140) energy is released as sound. And talking about sound, it's time to sound out this subject some more...

Explosive experiments fact file

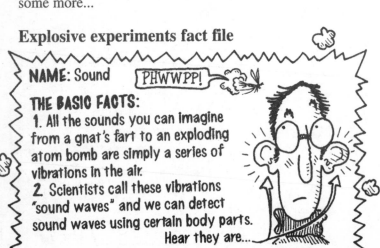

NAME: Sound PHWWPP!

THE BASIC FACTS:
1. All the sounds you can imagine from a gnat's fart to an exploding atom bomb are simply a series of vibrations in the air.
2. Scientists call these vibrations "sound waves" and we can detect sound waves using certain body parts.
Hear they are...

148

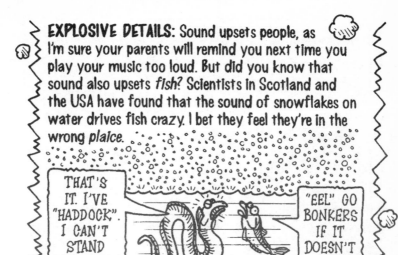

EXPLOSIVE DETAILS: Sound upsets people, as I'm sure your parents will remind you next time you play your music too loud. But did you know that sound also upsets *fish*? Scientists in Scotland and the USA have found that the sound of snowflakes on water drives fish crazy. I bet they feel they're in the wrong *plaice*.

THAT'S IT. I'VE "HADDOCK". I CAN'T STAND ANY MORE!

"EEL" GO BONKERS IF IT DOESN'T STOP!

Dare you discover ... sounds?

So you *like* the sound of noisy experiments? Well, you'll be pleased to hear that Wanda Wye has prepared some more experiments complete with quiz questions, and no, they don't involve deafening your pet goldfish. Wanda assures us that Bubbles is safe...

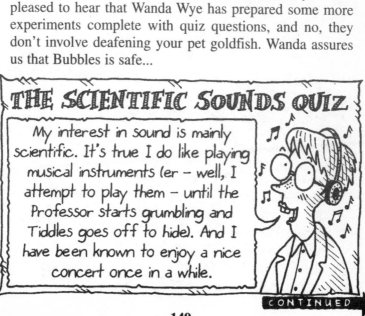

THE SCIENTIFIC SOUNDS QUIZ

My interest in sound is mainly scientific. It's true I do like playing musical instruments (er – well, I attempt to play them – until the Professor starts grumbling and Tiddles goes off to hide). And I have been known to enjoy a nice concert once in a while.

CONTINUED →

149

((('SALTY SOUND WAVES)))

WHAT YOU NEED:

A BOWL

SOME CLING FILM

SOME SALT

A RADIO

WHAT YOU DO:

OOER!

1 Cover the bowl with cling film. Make sure it's really tight – if you can play it like a drum then it's tight enough. Tiddles, don't look so scared – I'm not going to start drumming!

2 Sprinkle some salt over the cling film.

3 Switch on the radio and play some music a few centimetres away at full volume. Oops – sorry Professor, I didn't realize you were taking your afternoon nap!

WHAT DID YOU NOTICE?

ANSWER: The grains of salt dance on the cling film. That's because sound waves from the radio make the film vibrate.

⚠ HORRIBLE FAMILY WARNING!

Don't try this experiment at 5 a.m. or you might hear your teeth vibrating as you're shaken by your enraged parents.

SHOCKING SOUNDS

WHAT YOU NEED:

SOME COOKING OIL

A PIECE OF POLYSTYRENE

OR

A PIECE OF GLASS SUCH AS A BOWL, A MIRROR OR A WINDOW

WHAT YOU DO:

1 Slightly moisten the polystyrene.

2 Scrape the polystyrene over the glass.

3 Smear some oil over the glass and repeat step 2.

WHAT DID YOU NOTICE?

ANSWER: Do you like the squeaking noise at stage 2? The sound waves are made by the polystyrene catching tiny bumps in the glass and then springing away. Tiddles hated it – she raced outside and climbed to the top of a tall tree and I had to ring the fire brigade to rescue her. The noise sounds horrible to our ears (and the cat's) because the sound waves are unevenly spaced out (the sound waves of most music come at regular intervals). The oil allows the polystyrene to glide quietly over the glass. AHHH – that's better!

WITHOUT OIL

GLASS

WITH OIL

MEOW!

SQUEAK!

151

CONTINUED ➡

⚠ HORRIBLE FAMILY WARNING!

Don't make this sound whilst the rest of the family are watching telly or you might hear a few horrible squeaks of protest.

((((WEIRD WHINE)))) GLASSES

⚠ HORRIBLE DIFFICULTY WARNING!

This is a hard experiment so you may have to whine for adult help to get it right.

WHAT YOU NEED:

 SOME ←WATER

A FINGER (YOUR OWN)

A WINE GLASS

WHAT YOU DO:

1 Wash your hands and dry them carefully. (I took care to wash my hands. The Professor might not have been amused if he found mucky smears over his best wine glasses.)

2 Moisten your fingertip (no, not with spit – use water!) and stroke it lightly around the top of the rim of the glass. Your finger should be just touching the glass but not rubbing or pressing against it.

STROKE!

152

WHAT DID YOU NOTICE?

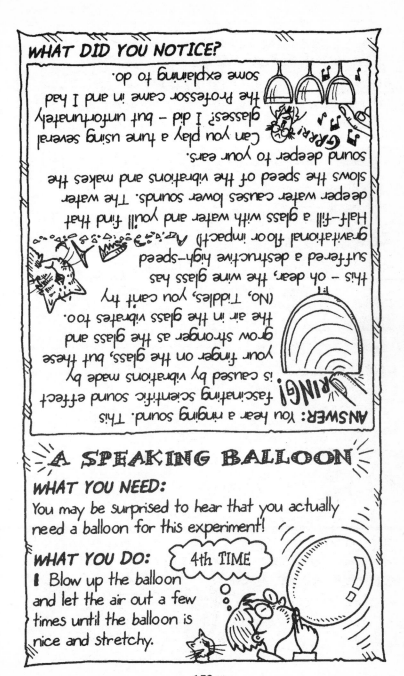

ANSWER: You hear a ringing sound. This fascinating scientific sound effect is caused by vibrations made by your finger on the glass, but these grow stronger as the glass and the air in the glass vibrates too. (No, Tiddles, you can't try this – oh dear, the wine glass has suffered a destructive high-speed gravitational floor impact!) Aeeeeee...

Half-fill a glass with water and you'll find that deeper water causes lower sounds. The water slows the speed of the vibrations and makes the sound deeper to your ears. Can you play a tune using several glasses? I did – but unfortunately the Professor came in and I had some explaining to do.

A SPEAKING BALLOON

WHAT YOU NEED:

You may be surprised to hear that you actually need a balloon for this experiment!

WHAT YOU DO:

1 Blow up the balloon and let the air out a few times until the balloon is nice and stretchy.

4th TIME

153

2 Blow up the balloon and hold the neck so that no air can get out.

3 Now pinch each side of the neck, and pull the sides apart.

PINCH!

WHAT DID YOU NOTICE?

ANSWER: You hear a squeaking noise and by pulling the neck wider and narrower you can play a tune! Your vocal cords work in the same way. They're found in your throat and change shape, shortening to make the higher sounds. Tiddles, get your claws off that balloon – oh ...!! Tiddles, don't be scared of the BANG! BANG! It's only a powerful sound wave!

Bet you never knew!
(Let's hope Tiddles doesn't read this bit!) In 1863 16-year-old scientist Alexander Graham Bell (1847-1922) decided to study how the vocal cords work. The family cat had just died, so he cut open its throat to examine its miaow-making bits. Don't try this on your pet cat – especially if it's still alive! Now, back to Wanda...

SLICE! TWANG!

HEAR HERE!

WHAT YOU NEED:

A WATCH

A SOUP BOWL

AN UMBRELLA. (I BORROWED THE PROFESSOR'S)

HORRIBLE FAMILY WARNING!

Putting up an umbrella indoors can damage fragile antiques and fatally damage your pocket money. **YOU HAVE BEEN WARNED!**

WHAT YOU DO:

1 Place the watch in the bowl and the bowl on the floor.

2 Stand over the bowl and put up the umbrella. Tiddles, stop sitting in the bowl and purring – you're spoiling the experiment!

3 Put your head on one side, close to the umbrella handle and block up the ear furthest from the umbrella.

TICK TOCK!

WHAT DID YOU NOTICE?

ANSWER: You can hear the watch ticking and the sound appears to come from the umbrella. That's brolly amazing, don't you think?

Sorry, I was trying to make a joke. In fact, the sound waves from the watch echo off the umbrella and WANDA'S into your ear. I've drawn a diagram to make things clearer: CONFUSED CAT

UMBRELLA

SOUND

WANDA'S EAR

BOWL

155

Bet you never knew!
Victorian vicar Rev John Blackburn built a giant sound reflector behind his pulpit to help people hear his sermons. Unfortunately, the reflector seems to have channelled all the sound towards one person sitting in the middle of the congregation, leaving everyone else no better off than before.

DON'T WORRY, YOU'RE NOT MISSING ANYTHING

Well, talking about hearing it all, I'm sure you think that you've heard all there is about sound and explosions. But there's a couple of effects of explosions that you probably haven't looked into. Any idea what they are? Well, the *buzz* in the next chapter is sure to shed some *light* on the mystery...

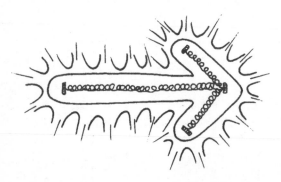

Yes, it's actually true, light and electricity are made by explosions. Look at this tasteful picture of a volcano blowing up and destroying an entire city...

SCIENTIFIC NOTE: The lightning is a giant electrical spark made by tiny bits of ash rubbing together (for more details see page 175). By the way, the only difference between lightning and electricity is that you don't have to pay for lightning, ha ha.

ELECTRICITY CAUSES LIGHTNING IN THE ASH CLOUD

LIGHT GLOWS FROM RED-HOT LAVA

So what's going on?

Well, let's begin with light. I'm sure these fascinating facts will shine a little light on the subject...

Explosive experiments fact file

NAME: Light

ATOM

THE BASIC FACTS:
1. The power to make light comes from electrons. These are tiny blips of energy that spend their time zipping around atoms. It's a wonder they don't get dizzy!

WE DO!

ELECTRON

2. The electrons let out light in the form of blips of energy called photons (tons). This happens when atoms are heated and try to cool down.

3. Obviously the atoms in the red hot lava are being heated quite a lot.

EXPLOSIVE DETAILS: Light is fast. I mean faster than a teacher chasing his wig on a windy day, faster than a gang of six year olds heading for a sweet shop, faster even than the school bully running to the toilet with a bad case of diarrhoea.

Yes, light is faster than anything in the known universe!

So how fast *is* light?

Well, to be exact it moves at 299,792,458 metres (186,282 miles) a second. Gobsmacked yet? You will be!

• Stand in the silvery moonlight and the light that falls on your face was on the moon's surface just 1.25 *seconds* ago.

• Sit in the sunshine and the hot sunlight that zaps your cheeks was on the surface of the sun just *eight minutes* ago.

• And if that doesn't make you feel a bit slow then consider this: photons don't just zoom in a straight line. They vibrate to and fro very, *very f-a-s-t*: over 400,000,000,000,000,000,000 (that's four hundred billion billion) times a second. (These speedy wiggles are known as light waves.)

Phew! Better sit down with a nice cold drink to get your energy back before this next bit of light relief...

Dare you discover ... light experiments?

It's an experiment quiz by light, electricity and magnetism scientist and inventor Professor Buzzoff. And don't worry – you're sure to make light work of the questions!

THE LIGHT QUIZ

I love light! It's so ordinary and yet so extraordinary – that's the beauty of it! Light appeals to both sides of me – the scientist and the artistic, sensitive side. Anyway, before I get carried away I'll wish you luck with these experiments!

ENVELOPE MYSTERY

WHAT YOU NEED:

A SELF-SEALING ENVELOPE (NOT ONE THAT YOU HAVE TO LICK).

A DARK ROOM

WHAT YOU DO:

1 Shut yourself in the dark room and close the envelope. **2** Wait until your eyes have got used to the dark. **3** Rip open the flap of the envelope as quickly as you can. (It took me several goes before anything happened. But then I saw it...)

WHAT DID YOU NOTICE?

ANSWER: You should see a mysterious flash. You used force to rip open the envelope flap and this force gives heat energy to the atoms of glue that hold the flap closed. Their electrons lose this energy in the form of light.

PHANTOM FACE

WHAT YOU NEED:

A **BRIGHT TORCH**

A MIRROR

A FRIEND (ONE OF MY SCIENTIFIC COLLEAGUES HELPED ME).

WHAT YOU DO:

1 Wait until dark and make sure the curtains are open. Hide in a corner of the room opposite the window.

2 Ask your friend to hold the mirror so it reflects light on to the window. You can work this out by shining your torch on to the mirror and watching to see where the light reflects.

3 Shine the torch on to your face from below and pull a horrible face. Stand so that the light from your face reflects on to the mirror.

WHAT DID YOU NOTICE?

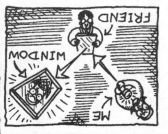

ANSWER: A ghostly face appears at the window – you'll probably spot it out of the corner of your eye. In fact, the light is reflected from your face to the mirror to the window and then back into the room.

161

CONTINUED ➡

HORRIBLE FAMILY WARNING!

You wouldn't do this to scare your little brother/sister would you? If so you'll have to "face" the consequences...

AGH!

THUMB SOME LIGHT

WHAT YOU NEED:

TWO THUMBS. (IT HELPS IF THEY'RE YOUR OWN.)

A LIGHT. (A BRIGHT WINDOW WILL DO)

WHAT YOU DO:

1 Put your thumbs together with the nails facing you. The thumbs should be just 3 mm (0.2 inches) apart.

2 Bring your thumbs up so that you're looking at the light through the gap between your thumbs. They should be about 5 cm (2 inches) from your face.

WHAT DID YOU NOTICE?

ANSWER: Thin lines appear between your thumbs. If you realized they were due to light you'll be on the right lines. (Sorry, that was a joke: just my artistic side trying to express itself!) The lines are

CONTINUED ➤

actually caused by light waves shining from different directions getting in each other's way and blotting each other out. I hope you like my drawing – it's rather artistic if I say so myself!

Now remember those lines because the Polish-born American astronomer in this next story spent years of his life trying to see them. His name was Albert Michelson (1852-1931) and he was trying to use light to find out about outer space. Here's his diary ... OK, it might just be a fake...

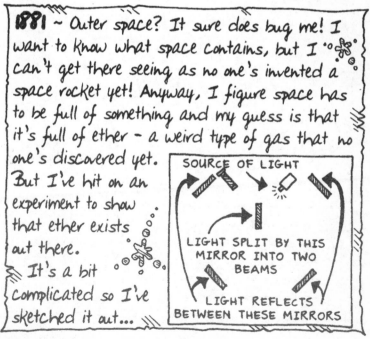

1881 ~ Outer space? It sure does bug me! I want to know what space contains, but I can't get there seeing as no one's invented a space rocket yet! Anyway, I figure space has to be full of something, and my guess is that it's full of ether – a weird type of gas that no one's discovered yet. But I've hit on an experiment to show that ether exists out there.

It's a bit complicated so I've sketched it out...

SOURCE OF LIGHT

LIGHT SPLIT BY THIS MIRROR INTO TWO BEAMS

LIGHT REFLECTS BETWEEN THESE MIRRORS

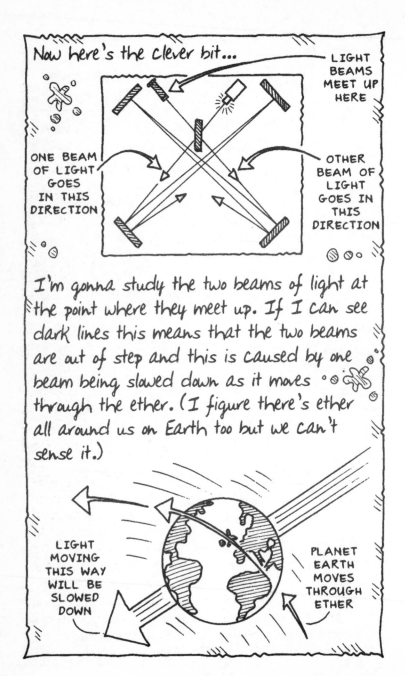

Now here's the clever bit...

LIGHT BEAMS MEET UP HERE

ONE BEAM OF LIGHT GOES IN THIS DIRECTION

OTHER BEAM OF LIGHT GOES IN THIS DIRECTION

I'm gonna study the two beams of light at the point where they meet up. If I can see dark lines this means that the two beams are out of step and this is caused by one beam being slowed down as it moves through the ether. (I figure there's ether all around us on Earth too but we can't sense it.)

LIGHT MOVING THIS WAY WILL BE SLOWED DOWN

PLANET EARTH MOVES THROUGH ETHER

Whoops! I should be saying "Thanks a million, buddy!" to my very rich scientific pal Alexander Graham Bell for giving me the cash to set up this experiment. Now to switch on the light and see those dark lines. So where are they? Drat! I can't see them anywhere! Oh well, I'll just have to set up everything again just in case a small mistake in positioning the mirrors has stopped me from seeing the lines.

GRRRR!

1887 ~ I've tried this experiment over one thousand times but I still can't see nothing! Nothing! Zilch! Not a sausage! Grr - I can't understand it. My machine can detect any slowing of the speed of light by 1 mm in 4000 km. So where's that pesky ether? I'm feeling really spaced out - but I'll keep on trying.

Michelson, helped by his friend Edward Morley (1838-1923, tried the experiment *thousands* of times. But he never saw any lines – I guess that was hard lines for him! He didn't see lines for a good reason: *there weren't any*! As scientist Albert Einstein realized in 1905, ether didn't exist. But you don't have to be Einstein to realize that this is what the experiment was telling the scientist.

So would you know the result of an experiment if it hit you in the face? Well, here's an exclusive peek at Professor Buzzoff's lab notebooks. Feel free to try some of her experiments yourself!

PROFESSOR BUZZOFF'S GREATEST EXPERIMENTS

by the Professor (that's me!)

Light, electricity and magnetism are fascinating electromagnetic phenomena and I often try these experiments for light relief. Yes, we scientists like to relax once in a while – I personally enjoy a little painting!

SCIENTIFIC NOTE

Scientists call the energy that makes light, electricity and magnetism, "electromagnetism" (e-leck-tro-mag-net-tism).

MIXED-UP COLOURS

WHAT I NEEDED:

A JAM-JAR

SOME OLIVE OIL

A RULER

SOME BLUE MOUTHWASH OR SOME WATER MIXED WITH THREE DROPS OF BLUE FOOD COLOUR

WHAT I DID:

1 I poured enough mouthwash to fill the jar to a depth of 5 cm (2 inches).

2 Then I poured on a layer of olive oil 0.5 cm (0.2 inches) thick – the oil floated on the mouthwash.

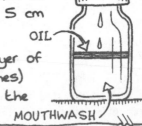

OIL

MOUTHWASH

3 I replaced the lid of the jar and shook it well and held the liquid up to the light.

RESULT: The liquid had turned green! After a few minutes, the yellow olive oil reappeared on top of the blue liquid.

REMARKS: Sunlight contains the colours in the rainbow. The colour of the oil and the mouthwash is due to their atoms only letting yellow and blue light through. When yellow and blue light is combined you get green light and that's what I saw. I should have poured the mixture away but I left it lying around. I later mistook it for salad dressing and put it on my lettuce. YUCK!

A GHOST OF A CHANCE

WHAT I NEEDED:

A BOX AT LEAST 12 CM WIDE x 17.5 CM LONG x 12 CM HIGH (4.7 INCHES x 7 INCHES).

A POSTCARD-SIZED PICTURE OF A GRAVEYARD OR RUIN. (I CUT THIS OUT OF A MAGAZINE BUT BEING A BIT OF AN ARTIST I'M GOING TO PAINT MY OWN SCENE. IT HAS TO BE 17.5 CM LONG AND 12 CM HIGH TO FIT THE BOX.)

A THIN LENGTH OF WIRE  (FLORIST'S WIRE IS IDEAL).

CONTINUED ➤

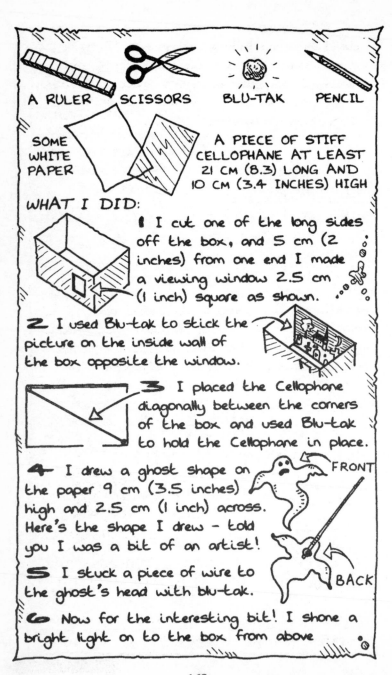

A RULER   SCISSORS   BLU-TAK   PENCIL

SOME WHITE PAPER

A PIECE OF STIFF CELLOPHANE AT LEAST 21 CM (8.3) LONG AND 10 CM (3.4 INCHES) HIGH

WHAT I DID:

1 I cut one of the long sides off the box, and 5 cm (2 inches) from one end I made a viewing window 2.5 cm (1 inch) square as shown.

2 I used Blu-tak to stick the picture on the inside wall of the box opposite the window.

3 I placed the Cellophane diagonally between the corners of the box and used Blu-tak to hold the Cellophane in place.

4 I drew a ghost shape on the paper 9 cm (3.5 inches) high and 2.5 cm (1 inch) across. Here's the shape I drew – told you I was a bit of an artist!

FRONT

5 I stuck a piece of wire to the ghost's head with blu-tak.

BACK

6 Now for the interesting bit! I shone a bright light on to the box from above (actually this wasn't vital because I could have put the box by a window). Then holding the wire, I dangled the ghost inside the box through the open top. I looked though the viewing window and saw...

RESULT: A see-though ghost glided amongst the graves and the ruins! Of course, there's no scientific basis for belief in ghosts but it's still a fascinating experiment.

REMARKS: This illusion is known as Pepper's ghost after the Victorian scientist who invented it. The light reflected off the ghost shape and on to the Cellophane. The Cellophane was see-through or "transparent" as we scientists say, and this makes the reflection of the ghost appear transparent.

PICTURE THIS!

WHAT I NEEDED:

A MAGNIFYING GLASS

A WHITE A4 PIECE OF PAPER

A WINDOW WITH DARK CURTAINS AND A BRIGHT SUNNY DAY OUTSIDE

WHAT I DID:

❦ I closed the curtains until only a thin stream of sunlight could get through.

CONTINUED ➡

2 I placed the paper on a table in front of the window.

3 Then I held the magnifying glass in front of the crack in the curtains and adjusted its position until light shone through the glass and on to the paper.

RESULT: A colour image of the view outside appeared on the paper - remarkable! I had to adjust the position of the glass, moving it a little nearer or a little further from the paper until the picture was in focus.

REMARKS: The lens of the magnifying glass bent the light coming from the scene outside on to the paper. The light was so bright that it made a picture.

SHOWER OF LIGHT

WHAT I NEEDED:

A JAM-JAR

A SHOWER WITH A HEAD THAT MOVED EASILY

A SMALL BRIGHT TORCH

A WASHING UP SPONGE

WHAT I DID:
■ I waited until dark.

2 I switched on the torch and placed it inside the jam jar with the beam pointing downwards. I pushed a dry sponge into the jar to hold the torch in position and replaced the lid.

3 Then I went into my bathroom and switched on the shower to a gentle stream. I switched off the light.

HORRIBLE MESS WARNING!

Only use the shower over the bath or shower tray — do not flood the bathroom or your parents will be in floods of tears.

HORRIBLE DANGER WARNING!

And never touch light switches with wet fingers or you might get a shock!

4 I held the shower head so that the water formed a fountain and held the jar under the shower-head so that the light shone upwards. Then I dropped the shower-head and got soaked — silly me!

WOW!

RESULT: The water from the shower turned into a fountain of light.

REMARKS: The light reflected inside each stream of water and made it glow.

CONTINUED ➔

171

> ## SCIENTIFIC NOTE
> This is how optical-fibre phonelines work. Your words are turned into pulses of laser light which reflect along inside the cables at the speed of light.
>
> And light is fast, remember, so it can keep up with the fastest talkers. The phone turns the light pulses into electric signals and then back into the sound of your friend chatting...

And talking about electrical signals, are you ready for some electrifying experiments?

Explosive experiments fact file

NAME: Magnetism and electricity

THE BASIC FACTS: 1 Remember the note on page 166? Magnetism and electricity are the same force – electromagnetism. Yes, say it in a science lesson and everyone will think you're a science genius!

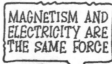

2 Normally the force spreads out from an atom in all directions and it's very weak. But in a magnet the metal atoms in the magnet form little boxes called domains. Lined up in this way, the force made by the electrons flows in one direction and becomes stronger.

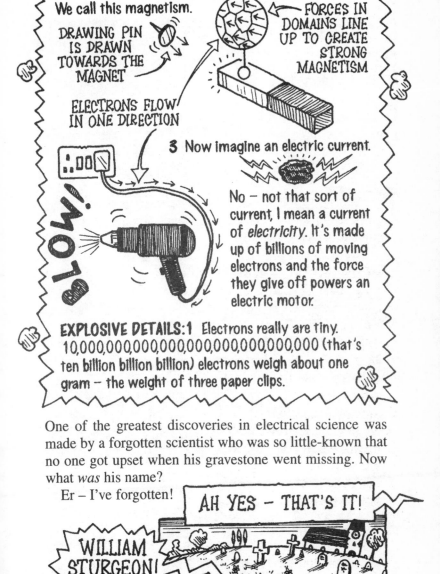

We call this magnetism.

DRAWING PIN IS DRAWN TOWARDS THE MAGNET

FORCES IN DOMAINS LINE UP TO CREATE STRONG MAGNETISM

ELECTRONS FLOW IN ONE DIRECTION

3 Now imagine an electric current.

No – not that sort of current, I mean a current of *electricity*. It's made up of billions of moving electrons and the force they give off powers an electric motor.

BLOW!

EXPLOSIVE DETAILS:1 Electrons really are tiny. 10,000,000,000,000,000,000,000,000,000,000 (that's ten billion billion billion) electrons weigh about one gram – the weight of three paper clips.

One of the greatest discoveries in electrical science was made by a forgotten scientist who was so little-known that no one got upset when his gravestone went missing. Now what *was* his name?

Er – I've forgotten!

AH YES – THAT'S IT!

WILLIAM STURGEON!

Hall of Fame: William Sturgeon (1783-1850)
Nationality: British

The rain fell in torrents and blew in wet sheets against the old grey stones of Devil's Bridge. The young lad shuddered in the chill wind and turned to the older man standing beside him under the bridge.

"We won't bag much tonight, Dad."

"You're right, lad," said the older man, shivering in his thin woollen coat. "May as well go 'ome, though you'll have to go to bed supperless as we've caught nowt for the pot."

"Wait, Dad," said the boy, "let's wait for the rain to slacken. At least we're sheltered 'ere."

Just then a massive bolt of lightning lit up the countryside and the white face of the boy as he flicked rainwater from his bedraggled hair. Then all went dark again.

"Wow!" breathed the boy, forgetting how cold and tired and hungry he was. "Look at all that electricity – I wonder where it comes from."

"From t'clouds, yer great silly!" said the man.

174

"Yes, Dad, but 'ow do clouds make it? When I grow up I'm going to find out all about electricity."

A terrific clap of thunder seemed to shake the old stones of the bridge. The man laughed.

"Don't be daft! You, a scientist! You're a poor cobbler's son with no book learning who 'as to go poaching to make ends meet."

There was a short silence broken only by the hissing of the rain and the roar of the water in the stream.

"I know that," said the boy, "but I'm going to do it some'ow." And his lips set in a thin, determined line.

And that, according to legend, is how young William Sturgeon decided to be a scientist and investigate electricity. Already people knew that lightning was a giant electrical spark but nobody was quite sure how the spark was made and whether the power of electricity could be harnessed to do work.

William joined the army as an ordinary soldier but he didn't forget his interest in electricity. He borrowed science books from the officers in return for mending their shoes, using skills his dad had taught him. On leaving the army, William decided to achieve his dream and study electricity but he found that he couldn't become a professor because he'd never been to school. (Yes, going to school does have its uses!)

So William tramped the countryside giving lectures about electricity and performing electrical experiments for money. Sometimes he was so poor that he went hungry and he was often soaked by the rain and snow.

But in 1823 William made an amazing discovery. He loved tinkering with electrical wires and batteries and he wrapped an electrical wire around a horseshoe. He switched on the current and the horseshoe became a powerful magnet – he had invented a device called an electromagnet.

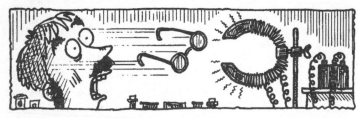

He used his new invention to make an electric motor that drove a metal shaft round and round.

The inventions earned William no money. People could see no use for the strange machines and the scientist continued to travel around giving lectures for a few pounds. Eventually he died and was buried in a humble grave and was quickly forgotten by the rest of the world.

But in the last hundred years scientists have discovered new uses for electromagnets and today they are found in the dynamos that produce electrical power and in electric motors that drive everything from CD players to washing machines and vacuum cleaners and fridges. If he was alive today William Sturgeon would be a multi-billionaire, but it all happened too late for him. He didn't even have his own gravestone because the cemetery gardener moved it and forgot where he put it.

Sometimes science can be *horribly* unfair!

So could you make a great discovery like William Sturgeon? Why not think it over as you make your very own electromagnet? You'll find full instructions in Professor Buzzoff's notebook...

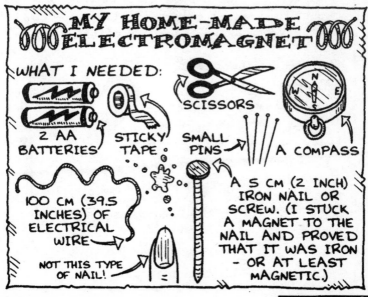

CONTINUED ➤

177

WHAT I DID:

1 I sticky-taped the ends of the two batteries together like so.

POSITIVE END →

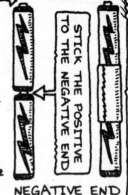

STICK THE POSITIVE TO THE NEGATIVE END

2 Then I stripped the plastic wrapping from the ends of the wire – 0.5 cm (0.15 inches) at each end – to expose the copper wire inside.

NEGATIVE END

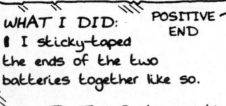

⚠️ HORRIBLE DANGER WARNING!

This requires a sharp knife. You *must* recruit an adult for wire-stripping or you might feel a bit cut up.

3 I used more sticky tape to stick one end of the wire to the positive end of the battery.

4 Next I wrapped the wire tightly around the entire length of the nail – and wrapped it around the length of the nail twice more.

5 Now I stuck the other end of the wire to the negative end of the battery.

6 I moved the wire backwards and forwards next to the compass.

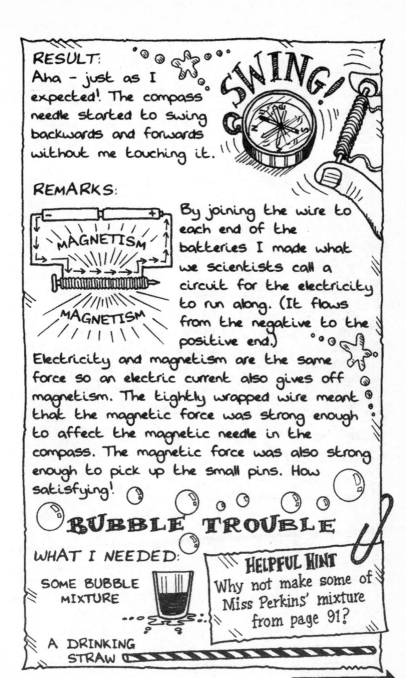

RESULT:
Aha – just as I expected! The compass needle started to swing backwards and forwards without me touching it.

SWING!

REMARKS:

MAGNETISM

MAGNETISM

By joining the wire to each end of the batteries I made what we scientists call a circuit for the electricity to run along. (It flows from the negative to the positive end.)

Electricity and magnetism are the same force so an electric current also gives off magnetism. The tightly wrapped wire meant that the magnetic force was strong enough to affect the magnetic needle in the compass. The magnetic force was also strong enough to pick up the small pins. How satisfying!

BUBBLE TROUBLE

WHAT I NEEDED:

SOME BUBBLE MIXTURE

A DRINKING STRAW

HELPFUL HINT
Why not make some of Miss Perkins' mixture from page 91?

179

CONTINUED

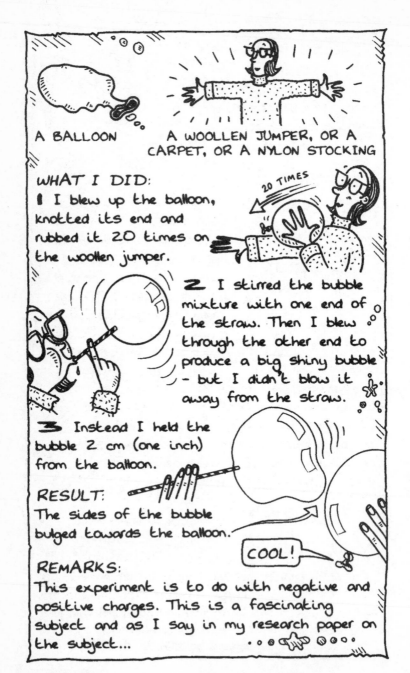

A BALLOON

A WOOLLEN JUMPER, OR A CARPET, OR A NYLON STOCKING

WHAT I DID:
1 I blew up the balloon, knotted its end and rubbed it 20 times on the woollen jumper.

20 TIMES

2 I stirred the bubble mixture with one end of the straw. Then I blew through the other end to produce a big shiny bubble – but I didn't blow it away from the straw.

3 Instead I held the bubble 2 cm (one inch) from the balloon.

RESULT:
The sides of the bubble bulged towards the balloon.

COOL!

REMARKS:
This experiment is to do with negative and positive charges. This is a fascinating subject and as I say in my research paper on the subject...

180

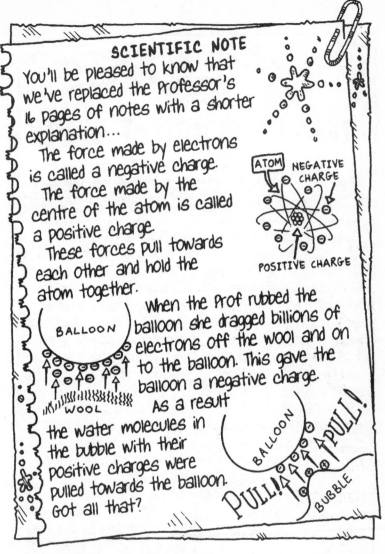

SCIENTIFIC NOTE

You'll be pleased to know that we've replaced the Professor's 16 pages of notes with a shorter explanation...

The force made by electrons is called a negative charge.

The force made by the centre of the atom is called a positive charge.

These forces pull towards each other and hold the atom together.

ATOM NEGATIVE CHARGE

POSITIVE CHARGE

BALLOON

WOOL

When the Prof rubbed the balloon she dragged billions of electrons off the wool and on to the balloon. This gave the balloon a negative charge.

As a result the water molecules in the bubble with their positive charges were pulled towards the balloon. Got all that?

PULL! PULL!

BALLOON

BUBBLE

So how did your experiments go?

Hopefully, you're not shocked by all these electricity experiments. But if you had tried the experiment in this next story you would have been shocked until your hair stood on end like a porcupine on a bad-hair day.

Yes, read on. It's a hair-raising tale...

COLORADO CLARION

—1901—

TESLA'S TERRIBLE TESTS!

World Exclusive!
by Harry J. Hacker, Chief Correspondent

Today the *Clarion* can exclusively reveal that the strange lightning flashes seen by Colorado Springs citizens were caused by science experiments.

As readers may know, local resident Nicola Tesla is famous for inventing a new type of electric motor.

But he became the subject of local gossip after a 200-foot aerial appeared above his laboratory. Then came last week's dramatic lightning displays.

We can now reveal that Tesla has been firing violent electric shocks deep into the Earth to make lightning. Tesla explained: "By launching the electric shocks at precisely the right intervals you build up a massive electrical surge that flows up the aerial and escapes to the clouds as lightning."

The scientist admitted that his New York lab burned down during similar tests but he offered the *Clarion* a demonstration.

"It's quite safe," he remarked, passing me a pair of rubber shoes with three-inch heels.

"But you'd best wear these in the lab – they block the electrical current – if you touched the ground whilst it's electrified you'd be frazzled alive."

The inventor flicked a switch and the giant electrical coils hummed into life and began growling like a deep-throated jungle beast. All around, wires buzzed and crackled. According to Tesla the shock waves were surging 6,000 feet underground and bouncing back. The air filled with humming and zapping.

"And now for the first lightning bolt!" shouted Tesla above the din. There was a loud crackle and the lab was suddenly lit with a brilliant flash of light that came from the glass panel in the ceiling. Lightning had blazed from the top of the aerial.

The entire building shook from the thunderclap released by the giant bolt of lightning.

Then suddenly all went dark.

"DRAT!" Tesla shouted.

I struck a match and saw the inventor was holding his head in his hands.

"I've burnt out the power station!" he moaned.

I promised him I'd tell the world about his work and made my excuses. I couldn't get out of there quick enough. Clearly Tesla is a great scientist but he's one helluva dangerous guy to have as a neighbour.

183

Bet you never knew!

In 1908 there was a huge, mysterious explosion in Tunguska in Siberia. Thousands of square kilometres of forest were flattened by the blast. Scientists think that it was caused by a bit of comet hitting Earth, but oddly enough a few months earlier Tesla had announced that he had invented a death ray and he would test it near the North Pole. Coincidence? Well, by then Tesla was a crazy old man who made all kinds of wild claims. But some people believe that Tunguska was Tesla's most explosive experiment...

One thing is certain, experiments are changing our world big time and they could have explosive effects on *your* future. So, if you want to know what tomorrow holds for you today, you'd best read the next chapter right *now*!

EPILOGUE: AN EXPLOSIVE TOMORROW?

But before we move on to the future, let's take a quick look back at the weird, wild, wacky and explosive world of experiments.

Some experiments are big and loud, and others are tiny and make less sound than a squeaky little mouse. And experimenters can be very brave ... or are they just fooling themselves...?

Very brave (or should we say foolish?) experimenters

Scientists Pierre and Marie Curie (1859-1906 and 1867-1934) were fascinated by radioactivity and they found two previously unknown radioactive substances, radium and polonium.

Explosive expressions

Answer: NO! Radioactivity is the way that certain types of atoms fall apart over time. The atoms break up because they gradually lose energy in the form of light and high energy rays.

Pierre Curie wanted to know what radioactivity would do to the skin so he tried a dangerous experiment. Here's what his lab notes might have said...

186

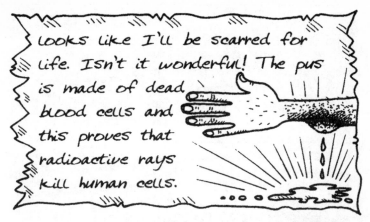

Looks like I'll be scarred for life. Isn't it wonderful! The pus is made of dead blood cells and this proves that radioactive rays kill human cells.

It's lucky Curie didn't swallow the radium – he'd have got atomic ache then! But whilst some scientists were being stupidly brave in their experiments, other scientists were being ... well ... stupidly stupid.

An experimenter who was fooling himself...

Let's imagine that science TV programmes were around in 1906.

Sickening Flickers

SCIENCE TODAY

Welcome to Science Today with all the latest science news!

With me is French scientist, René-Prosper Blondlot and American Professor Robert Williams Wood.

Bonjour!

Howdy!

Wood was right – Blondlot was wrong. Blondlot was desperate to discover a new kind of ray and he imagined effects that weren't really there. Further tests proved that N-rays didn't exist. The failed experiment wrecked Blondlot's entire life. He gave up his job and lived out the rest of his days as a poor and miserable old man.

So what about the future?

Today, scientists are trying more experiments than ever and some of these tests could have big effects on our lives. For example, Japanese scientists have developed chewing gum with chemicals that can boost your memory.

This sounds really important and I'd like to tell you more but ... er … I can't remember the details.

In 2000, scientists in Princeton, USA, sent a beam of light through a cloud of gas called caesium (sees-e-um) *faster* than light travels through space. As a result they saw the light leaving the cloud before they saw it enter the cloud. That's *weird*! Imagine seeing yourself leave school before you'd even walked through the door!

But this discovery won't lead to shorter school days – that really would be breaking the laws of science!

Meanwhile Chinese scientists have found how to make power from sewage by removing explosive hydrogen gas

189

and burning it. You might poo-poo this idea, but in a few years the contents of your toilet could be heating your home. (How's that for a chain reaction!)

And whilst we're on the subject of the future, here's how experiments could be re-shaping our future...

Future medicine/biology
Most of the exciting experiments in medicine and biology will be about genes (see page 75 if you think that genes are trousers with a washed 'n' faded look). After cracking the human genetic code in 2000 scientists are trying to find out what these genes actually do to our bodies and this could mean inserting human genes into the cells of animals to see what happens. Meanwhile, biologists will be studying the genes of animals to see how they work. And this info will help scientists develop new gene-based medicines that could replace damaged genes in the body.

Future chemistry
Scientists in Germany and the USA are working on supercomputers that can predict the result of chemistry experiments. The programs contain the results of hundreds of thousands of reactions where the results are known and can use this info to tell scientists the likely effects of combining

similar chemicals. But I'm sorry to say that these computers will *not* be available to help with your science homework!

Future physics

Physics is the science that deals with forces and energy – things like magnetism, light and electricity. (Professor Large, Wanda Wye and Professor Buzzoff are all happy to be called physicists.) And physicists are fascinated by weird topics like what atoms are made of and the existence of black holes in space. In future, physicists might make a black hole here on Earth, but some people worry that if things went wrong the black hole would scoff our planet! Most scientists would scoff at these fears...

191

We can't be sure what scientists will discover next and which experiments will produce great discoveries. But one thing is certain: experiments are the most powerful method humans have ever devised for solving the mysteries of life, the world and the universe. Mind you, scientists will never explain *everything*. You see, a good experiment highlights new questions that need to be answered by – yes, you guessed it – *more* experiments!

Science is an endless journey into the unknown and experiments are like lamps that show the way further and further into the dark. And if you think that sounds horribly frustrating and horribly mysterious, you're right. It is.

But it's also horribly exciting and horribly amazing and even horribly funny. Oh well, I guess that's Horrible Science for you!